LIVE LIFE
Beautifully
365 days of ideas & inspiration

GOOD
HOUSEKEEPING

2022

PHASES OF THE MOON:

● New moon   ◐ First quarter   ○ Full moon   ◑ Last quarter

This calendar is intended as a reference volume only, not as a medical manual. The information given here is designed to help you make informed decisions about your health. It is not intended as a substitute for any treatment that may have been prescribed by your doctor. If you suspect that you have a medical problem, we urge you to seek competent medical help.

Mention of specific companies, organizations, or authorities in this book does not imply endorsement by the author or publisher, nor does mention of specific companies, organizations, or authorities imply that they endorse this book, its author, or the publisher. Internet addresses and telephone numbers given in this book were accurate at the time it went to press.

Printed in China

Calendar design by Carol Angstadt
Photo editing by Monica Matthews
Photo credits can be found on the last page of the calendar.

ISBN-978-1-950099-86-3 hardcover
2   4   6   8   10   9   7   5   3   1   hardcover

HEARST

2021

SEPTEMBER
S	M	T	W	T	F	S
			1	2	3	4
5	6	7	8	9	10	11
12	13	14	15	16	17	18
19	20	21	22	23	24	25
26	27	28	29	30		

OCTOBER
S	M	T	W	T	F	S
					1	2
3	4	5	6	7	8	9
10	11	12	13	14	15	16
17	18	19	20	21	22	23
24	25	26	27	28	29	30
31						

NOVEMBER
S	M	T	W	T	F	S
	1	2	3	4	5	6
7	8	9	10	11	12	13
14	15	16	17	18	19	20
21	22	23	24	25	26	27
28	29	30				

DECEMBER
S	M	T	W	T	F	S
			1	2	3	4
5	6	7	8	9	10	11
12	13	14	15	16	17	18
19	20	21	22	23	24	25
26	27	28	29	30	31	

2022

JANUARY
S	M	T	W	T	F	S
						1
2	3	4	5	6	7	8
9	10	11	12	13	14	15
16	17	18	19	20	21	22
23	24	25	26	27	28	29
30	31					

FEBRUARY
S	M	T	W	T	F	S
		1	2	3	4	5
6	7	8	9	10	11	12
13	14	15	16	17	18	19
20	21	22	23	24	25	26
27	28					

MARCH
S	M	T	W	T	F	S
		1	2	3	4	5
6	7	8	9	10	11	12
13	14	15	16	17	18	19
20	21	22	23	24	25	26
27	28	29	30	31		

APRIL
S	M	T	W	T	F	S
					1	2
3	4	5	6	7	8	9
10	11	12	13	14	15	16
17	18	19	20	21	22	23
24	25	26	27	28	29	30

MAY
S	M	T	W	T	F	S
1	2	3	4	5	6	7
8	9	10	11	12	13	14
15	16	17	18	19	20	21
22	23	24	25	26	27	28
29	30	31				

JUNE
S	M	T	W	T	F	S
			1	2	3	4
5	6	7	8	9	10	11
12	13	14	15	16	17	18
19	20	21	22	23	24	25
26	27	28	29	30		

JULY
S	M	T	W	T	F	S
					1	2
3	4	5	6	7	8	9
10	11	12	13	14	15	16
17	18	19	20	21	22	23
24	25	26	27	28	29	30
31						

AUGUST
S	M	T	W	T	F	S
	1	2	3	4	5	6
7	8	9	10	11	12	13
14	15	16	17	18	19	20
21	22	23	24	25	26	27
28	29	30	31			

SEPTEMBER
S	M	T	W	T	F	S
				1	2	3
4	5	6	7	8	9	10
11	12	13	14	15	16	17
18	19	20	21	22	23	24
25	26	27	28	29	30	

OCTOBER
S	M	T	W	T	F	S
						1
2	3	4	5	6	7	8
9	10	11	12	13	14	15
16	17	18	19	20	21	22
23	24	25	26	27	28	29
30	31					

NOVEMBER
S	M	T	W	T	F	S
		1	2	3	4	5
6	7	8	9	10	11	12
13	14	15	16	17	18	19
20	21	22	23	24	25	26
27	28	29	30			

DECEMBER
S	M	T	W	T	F	S
				1	2	3
4	5	6	7	8	9	10
11	12	13	14	15	16	17
18	19	20	21	22	23	24
25	26	27	28	29	30	31

2023

JANUARY
S	M	T	W	T	F	S
1	2	3	4	5	6	7
8	9	10	11	12	13	14
15	16	17	18	19	20	21
22	23	24	25	26	27	28
29	30	31				

FEBRUARY
S	M	T	W	T	F	S
			1	2	3	4
5	6	7	8	9	10	11
12	13	14	15	16	17	18
19	20	21	22	23	24	25
26	27	28				

MARCH
S	M	T	W	T	F	S
			1	2	3	4
5	6	7	8	9	10	11
12	13	14	15	16	17	18
19	20	21	22	23	24	25
26	27	28	29	30	31	

APRIL
S	M	T	W	T	F	S
						1
2	3	4	5	6	7	8
9	10	11	12	13	14	15
16	17	18	19	20	21	22
23	24	25	26	27	28	29
30						

SEPTEMBER 2021

MONDAY	TUESDAY	WEDNESDAY	THURSDAY
		1	**2**
6 Labor Day Rosh Hashanah ●	**7**	**8**	**9**
13 ◑	**14**	**15** Yom Kippur Begins	**16**
20 ○	**21**	**22** First Day of Fall	**23**
27	**28**	**29**	**30**

FRIDAY	SATURDAY	SUNDAY
3	**4**	**5**
10	**11**	**12**
17	**18**	**19**
24	**25**	**26**

≡ **HOME HACK** ≡

Use your ceiling fan to stay comfy during in-between weather. Set the blades to spin clockwise to cool down and the other way to warm up.

AUGUST

M	T	W	T	F	S	S
						1
2	3	4	5	6	7	8
9	10	11	12	13	14	15
16	17	18	19	20	21	22
23	24	25	26	27	28	29
30	31					

OCTOBER

M	T	W	T	F	S	S
				1	2	3
4	5	6	7	8	9	10
11	12	13	14	15	16	17
18	19	20	21	22	23	24
25	26	27	28	29	30	31

OCTOBER 2021

MONDAY	TUESDAY	WEDNESDAY	THURSDAY
4	5	6 ●	7
11 Indigenous Peoples' Day	12	13 ◐	14
18	19	20 ○	21
25	26	27	28 ◑

FRIDAY	SATURDAY	SUNDAY
1	**2**	**3**
8	**9**	**10**
15	**16**	**17**
22	**23**	**24**
29	**30**	**31** Halloween

notes

_____
_____
_____
_____
_____
_____
_____
_____
_____

≈ **KITCHEN** ≈
HACK
To get broken eggshells out of a bowl of eggs, dip your clean finger in some water and the piece of shell with easily adhere to your finger.

SEPTEMBER

M	T	W	T	F	S	S
		1	2	3	4	5
6	7	8	9	10	11	12
13	14	15	16	17	18	19
20	21	22	23	24	25	26
27	28	29	30			

NOVEMBER

M	T	W	T	F	S	S
1	2	3	4	5	6	7
8	9	10	11	12	13	14
15	16	17	18	19	20	21
22	23	24	25	26	27	28
29	30					

NOVEMBER 2021

MONDAY	TUESDAY	WEDNESDAY	THURSDAY
1 All Saints' Day	**2**	**3**	**4** Diwali ●
8	**9**	**10**	**11** Veterans Day ◑
15	**16**	**17**	**18**
22	**23**	**24**	**25** Thanksgiving
29	**30**		

FRIDAY	SATURDAY	SUNDAY
5	**6**	**7** Daylight Savings Time Ends
12	**13**	**14**
19 ○	**20**	**21**
26	**27** ◑	**28** First Sunday of Advent Hanukkah Begins

notes

_____
_____
_____
_____
_____
_____
_____
_____
_____
_____
_____

≒ **LIFE** ≒
HACK
Beat the Thanksgiving grocery rush by shopping on a weekday morning, soon after the stores open. The aisles are more likely to be restocked and uncrowded.

OCTOBER

M	T	W	T	F	S	S
			1	2	3
4	5	6	7	8	9	10
11	12	13	14	15	16	17
18	19	20	21	22	23	24
25	26	27	28	29	30	31

DECEMBER

M	T	W	T	F	S	S
		1	2	3	4	5
6	7	8	9	10	11	12
13	14	15	16	17	18	19
20	21	22	23	24	25	26
27	28	29	30	31		

DECEMBER 2021

MONDAY	TUESDAY	WEDNESDAY	THURSDAY
		1	2
6	7	8	9
13	14	15	16
20 ○	21 First Day of Winter	22	23
27	28 ●	29	30

FRIDAY	SATURDAY	SUNDAY
3	**4** ●	**5**
10 ◑	**11**	**12**
17	**18** ○	**19**
24 Christmas Eve	**25** Christmas Day	**26** First Day of Kwanzaa ◑
31 New Year's Eve		

notes

_____

_____

_____

_____

_____

_____

_____

_____

_____

⊰ **HOLIDAY HACK** ⊱

Start a new family tradition by spreading good cheer volunteering together at a holiday meal or gift give-away for families in need.

NOVEMBER

M	T	W	T	F	S	S
1	2	3	4	5	6	7
8	9	10	11	12	13	14
15	16	17	18	19	20	21
22	23	24	25	26	27	28
29	30					

JANUARY

M	T	W	T	F	S	S
					1	2
3	4	5	6	7	8	9
10	11	12	13	14	15	16
17	18	19	20	21	22	23
24	25	26	27	28	29	30
31						

Welcome to
YOUR YEAR OF CALM

Your goal in 2022: Spend less time on things that leave you feeling frazzled so you have more time for joy. Use these handy checklists to help organize your life and prioritize self-care, and reaching it will be a snap.

DAILY

refresh

- ◯ Meditate for 5 minutes
- ◯ Take time to stretch
- ◯ _____
- ◯ _____

simplify

- ◯ Make your bed
- ◯ Clear kitchen counters
- ◯ _____
- ◯ _____

plan

- ◯ Refill your water bottle hourly
- ◯ Decide tomorrow's meals
- ◯ _____
- ◯ _____

connect

- ◯ Write down one thing you're grateful for
- ◯ Have a meaningful conversation
- ◯ _____
- ◯ _____

other

- ◯ _____
- ◯ _____

CHECKLIST

WEEKLY

refresh
- ⭕ Take a long walk
- ⭕ Enjoy a nap
- ⭕ _____
- ⭕ _____

simplify
- ⭕ Pick a space to tidy up
- ⭕ Pack grab-and-go snacks to stay healthy
- ⭕ _____
- ⭕ _____

plan
- ⭕ Review calendar for upcoming appointments
- ⭕ Map out meals for the week
- ⭕ _____
- ⭕ _____

connect
- ⭕ Call a friend
- ⭕ Pay it forward
- ⭕ _____
- ⭕ _____

other
- ⭕ _____
- ⭕ _____

refresh
- ○ Enjoy a spa day at home
- ○ Read a book
- ○ _____
- ○ _____

simplify
- ○ Clean out the fridge
- ○ Clean out your email inbox
- ○ _____
- ○ _____

plan
- ○ Delegate a chore
- ○ Make a new goal to reach for
- ○ _____
- ○ _____

connect
- ○ Have lunch with a friend
- ○ Volunteer your time
- ○ _____
- ○ _____

other
- ○ _____
- ○ _____

★

CHECKLIST

WINTER

refresh
- ○ Bundle up and get outside
- ○ Sip an herbal tea
- ○ _____
- ○ _____

simplify
- ○ Check medicine cabinet for expired items
- ○ Try an online grocery delivery service
- ○ _____
- ○ _____

plan
- ○ Buy garden seeds
- ○ Research summer vacation options
- ○ _____
- ○ _____

connect
- ○ Organize a game night
- ○ Host a potluck
- ○ _____
- ○ _____

other
- ○ _____
- ○ _____

SPRING

refresh

○ Buy a new outfit in a color you love

○ Enjoy a pedicure

○ _____

○ _____

simplify

○ Wash your windows

○ Deep-clean carpets and floors

○ _____

○ _____

plan

○ Gather tax documents

○ Back up your computer and phone

○ _____

○ _____

connect

○ Find an exercise buddy

○ Plan a movie night at home with a friend

○ _____

○ _____

other

○ _____

○ _____

CHECKLIST

SUMMER

refresh
- ○ Try a new hairstyle
- ○ Enjoy a beach read
- ○ _____
- ○ _____

simplify
- ○ Invest in car organizers
- ○ Hang a hammock and relax
- ○ _____
- ○ _____

plan
- ○ Organize a yard sale
- ○ Pack a "go bag" for spontaneous travel
- ○ _____
- ○ _____

connect
- ○ Pack a picnic to share with a loved one
- ○ Send a postcard to a friend far away
- ○ _____
- ○ _____

other
- ○ _____
- ○ _____

★
CHECKLIST
FALL

refresh
- ○ Book a massage appointment
- ○ Take a mental health day
- ○ _____
- ○ _____

simplify
- ○ Stock up on new gloves, hats and scarves
- ○ Donate old clothes
- ○ _____
- ○ _____

plan
- ○ Schedule flu shots
- ○ Reorganize your pantry
- ○ _____
- ○ _____

connect
- ○ Sign up for a class and learn something new
- ○ Visit with someone who could use the company
- ○ _____
- ○ _____

other
- ○ _____
- ○ _____

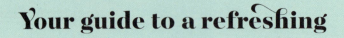

Your guide to a refreshing

WINTER

Don't let the cold, dark months get you down! These easy little mood- and health-boosting to-do's will turn them into your own personal season of renewal and growth.

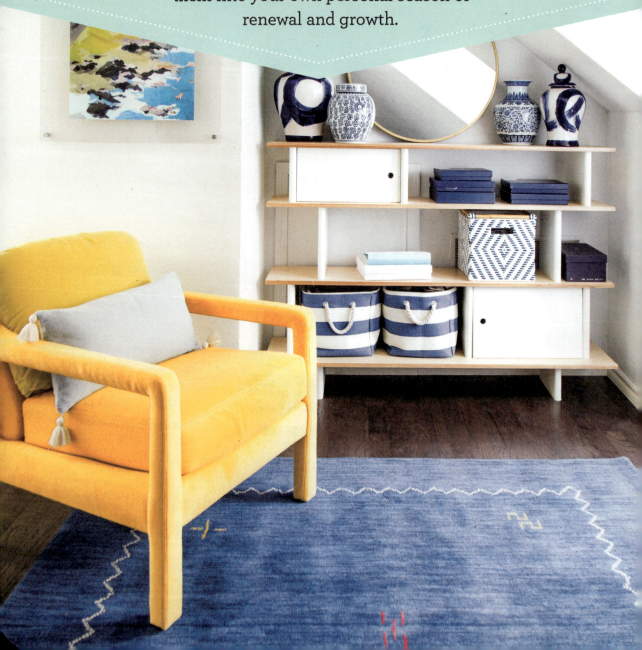

SURROUND YOURSELF WITH
Joyful Colors

Rachel Shingleton, the Oklahoma-based design genius behind the popular blog *Lover of the Color Blue* and Instagram @pencilshavings, has never met a color she didn't love: "I grew up in a home decorated in the most saturated shades of blue and green, so I gravitate toward them," she says.

Let a shade you love set the tone (literally) for a happy house. It can boost your mood considerably. Here are some ideas to consider:

WALLPAPER A SMALL SPACE IN A BIG PRINT. A hallway is a great place to make a statement, and a bright pop of pattern can make you feel happy when you walk in the door.

FOCUS ON LITTLE BURSTS. Can't commit to a permanent pattern, or don't want allover color? Add fun and pretty statement accessories.

REUSE, REPURPOSE, RE-COVER! If you want to experiment with a new shade, why not upcycle something you already own? It's a great low-risk and budget-friendly way to give new life to an old furnishing, and you might enjoy the new look even more.

Squash Stress Fast

Need to take a moment for yourself? Make it count with these simple strategies.

STRETCH YOURSELF. You don't even need to own a yoga mat, let alone be physically flexible, to reap the benefits of the ancient practice of yoga. There's a ton of research on its role in stress reduction, and taking even 10 minutes to breathe and stretch in any way that feels good to you can be incredibly soothing. Check out the apps Glo and Pocket Yoga, and if the weather cooperates, do your moves outside so you can take some fresh air into your lungs while you do happy baby pose.

MEDITATE—OR EVEN JUST BREATHE CONSCIOUSLY. This is another well-researched stress-relieving practice that some people are intimidated by but that is simple and effective once you do it, even for 2 minutes. Forget about the clearing-your-mind thing and focus on breathing. Research has shown slow breathing to have calming effects on the central nervous system and the cardiovascular system, and a recent study from China found that belly breathing might improve attention, mood and levels of the stress hormone cortisol. Try guided meditations on the apps Calm and UnPlug, or set a timer for a minute or two and just sit and breathe deeply from your diaphragm.

ENJOY A CALMING BATH

One of the best ways to reduce stress is to surround yourself with a relaxing physical environment, like a warm bath, says George Slavich, Ph.D., a clinical psychologist and director of the Laboratory for Stress Assessment and Research at UCLA. For maximum benefits, add a skin-soothing ingredient such as chamomile or oatmeal to the water before soaking, suggests Elizabeth Trattner, a wellness expert in Miami.

LAB PICKS Pour or sprinkle in a premade oatmeal- or chamomile-based foam bath, such as **Dr Teal's** Comfort & Calm Foaming Bath, or salts. Or "brew" a bath with one of the new tub teas, like **Treets Traditions** Bath Tea—they're blends of botanicals commonly found in tea that infuse your bath with aromatherapy and skincare properties.

DIY
TUB TEA

4 chamomile tea bags
1 cup warm water

Steep tea bags in a container filled with water for 5 minutes, then use a spoon to push the bags against the side to extract more chamomile, Trattner says. Pour the tea into a bathtub filled with warm water and mix before entering.

HYDRATE INSIDE AND OUT

Dehydration decreases the volume of blood that flows to the skin, making you look "pale and sickly," explains skincare expert Tammie Umbel, founder of Shea Terra Organics. It may seem like a short-term problem solved by a glass of water, but Janet Prystowsky, M.D., Ph.D., a dermatologist in New York City, encourages viewing skin dehydration over the long term. A consistent lack of hydration can cause lasting damage like fine lines, sagging skin and even scaliness from severe chronic dehydration.

THE FIX: Drink up! Aim for at least 8 cups per day of water or other sugar- and caffeine-free beverages like naturally flavored seltzers, recommends the Good Housekeeping Institute's registered dietitian nutritionist, Stefani Sassos.

If you want to determine the exact amount you should drink according to your body weight, you can follow these steps:

1 Take your weight (in pounds) and divide that by 2.2.

2 Multiply that number depending on your age: If you're younger than 30, multiply by 40. If you're between 30 and 55, multiply by 35. If you're older than 55, multiply by 30.

3 Divide that sum by 28.3.

4 Your total is how many ounces of water you should drink each day. Divide that number by 8 to see your result in cups.

Spice Up an Old Fave

INSTANT POT CHICKEN PHO

Active **20 min.** | Total **1 hr.**

If you're itching to move in a new direction but still craving comfort, this classic Vietnamese soup is the perfect solution. Loaded with fresh flavors, it will wake up your senses while still reminding you of a familiar favorite.

- 4 star anise pods
- 4 cloves
- 1 small cinnamon stick, smashed
- 1 tsp coriander seeds, crushed
- ½ tsp black peppercorns
- 1 2-in. piece ginger, quartered and then smashed
- ½ red onion, coarsely chopped
- ½ Fuji apple
- 1½ lbs chicken thighs, skin removed
- 2 Tbsp fish sauce, divided
- 3 oz instant rice noodles
  Bean sprouts, sliced red chile, red onion, mint or cilantro and lime wedges, for serving

1. Press Sauté on Instant Pot. Add star anise, cloves, cinnamon, coriander and peppercorns and sauté until fragrant, 3 to 4 min.

2. Add ginger and onion and cook, stirring occasionally, 4 min. Add apple, chicken, 5 cups water and 1 Tbsp fish sauce; cover and lock lid. Cook on high pressure 22 min. Use natural release for 10 min., then release any remaining pressure.

3. Transfer chicken to plate. Strain broth, discarding remaining solids. Return broth to pot, add noodles and let sit until tender, 3 to 4 min.

4. Meanwhile, shred chicken, discarding bones. Return to pot and stir in remaining 1 Tbsp fish sauce. Serve with desired toppings.

SERVES 4 About 235 cal, 5 g fat (1.5 g sat), 23 g pro, 730 mg sodium, 22 g carb, 0 g fiber

AN INSTANT POT is a handy tool for creating intensely flavored soups, but if you don't have one, simply simmer all the ingredients called for in the first two steps in a large covered stockpot for about an hour.

JANUARY 2022

MONDAY	TUESDAY	WEDNESDAY	THURSDAY
3	4	5	6
10	11	12	13
17 Martin Luther King Jr. Day ○	18	19	20
24	25 ○	26	27
31			

FRIDAY	SATURDAY	SUNDAY
	1 New Year's Day	**2** ●
7	**8**	**9** ◑
14	**15**	**16**
21	**22**	**23**
28	**29**	**30**

FIND TIME FOR FITNESS

. . . even if it's just a little bit of time. **Short bursts of movement are great** if tension is making you feel jittery. It doesn't matter if it's 20 jumping jacks, 10 push-ups or sit-ups or a quick jog around the block. "A burst of activity gets your heart rate up and, even if brief, will activate several neurotransmitters (including dopamine, serotonin and norepinephrine) that enhance your mood and help cushion some of that anxiety," says Guillem Gonzalez-Lomas, M.D., an orthopedic surgeon at NYU Langone Sports Health.

DECEMBER

M	T	W	T	F	S	S
		1	2	3	4	5
6	7	8	9	10	11	12
13	14	15	16	17	18	19
20	21	22	23	24	25	26
27	28	29	30	31		

FEBRUARY

M	T	W	T	F	S	S
	1	2	3	4	5	6
7	8	9	10	11	12	13
14	15	16	17	18	19	20
21	22	23	24	25	26	27
28						

M	T	W	T	F	S	S
27	28	29	30	31	1	2
3	4	5	6	7	8	9
10	11	12	13	14	15	16
17	18	19	20	21	22	23
24	25	26	27	28	29	30
31						

"You never fail until you stop trying."

—ALBERT EINSTEIN

27 MONDAY

28 TUESDAY

29 WEDNESDAY

30 THURSDAY

31 FRIDAY

1 SATURDAY New Year's Day

2 SUNDAY ●

JANUARY 3–9
2022

M	T	W	T	F	S	S
					1	2
3	4	5	6	7	8	9
10	11	12	13	14	15	16
17	18	19	20	21	22	23
24	25	26	27	28	29	30
31						

Grease Your Hinges

When it comes to keeping your joints working smoothly, it's said that "motion is lotion." An ideal joint-boosting routine combines 150 minutes a week of moderate aerobic exercise such as fast walking or biking with a couple of sessions of strength training such as with free weights or resistance bands. Try these small daily moves too.

IMPROVE YOUR BALANCE. "Proprioception is information going from your joints to your brain and then to your muscles so they contract and you don't fall over," says Dr. Pierce-Talsma, D.O., M.S., an associate dean at the University of New England College of Osteopathic Medicine. To better your proprioception, try standing on one leg, then the other, for a minute each while you brush your teeth every day.

DON'T JUST SIT THERE. Long sessions hunched in front of a computer are a recipe for stiffness. Take regular breaks to keep joints lubricated. Maura Daly Iversen, D.P.T., S.D., a professor of public health and physical therapy at Sacred Heart University in Fairfield, CT, suggests setting a timer to remind yourself every 30 minutes to walk around or march in place.

3 MONDAY

4 TUESDAY

5 WEDNESDAY

6 THURSDAY

7 FRIDAY

8 SATURDAY

9 SUNDAY ◑

JANUARY 10–16

2022

M	T	W	T	F	S	S
					1	2
3	4	5	6	7	8	9
10	11	12	13	14	15	16
17	18	19	20	21	22	23
24	25	26	27	28	29	30
31						

Pump Iron . . . the Tasty Way

Power through long days with this easy sheet pan dish. Shellfish and other iron-rich foods improve oxygen flow throughout your body so you can feel more energized.

SHEET PAN SHRIMP & ZOODLES

Active **10 min.** | Total **25 min.**

- 1 lb spiralized zucchini
- 2 Tbsp olive oil, divided
  Salt and pepper
- 4 scallions, thinly sliced
- 4 cloves garlic, thinly sliced
- 1 small red chile, thinly sliced
- 2 Tbsp dry white wine
- 1 Tbsp fresh lemon juice
- 20 pieces large shrimp, peeled and deveined
- 4 oz crumbled feta

1. Heat oven to 475°F. On large, rimmed baking sheet, toss spiralized zucchini with 1 Tbsp olive oil and ¼ tsp each salt and pepper; arrange in an even layer and roast 6 min.
2. Meanwhile, in large bowl, combine scallions, garlic, chile, white wine, lemon juice and ¼ tsp each salt and pepper. Add shrimp and toss to coat.
3. Scatter shrimp over zucchini, drizzle with 1 Tbsp oil and sprinkle with crumbled feta. Roast until shrimp are opaque throughout, 5 to 7 min.

SERVES 4 About 200 cal, 13.5 g fat (5.5 g sat), 11 g pro, 715 mg sodium, 10 g carb, 2 g fiber

10 MONDAY

11 TUESDAY

12 WEDNESDAY

13 THURSDAY

14 FRIDAY

15 SATURDAY

16 SUNDAY

JANUARY 17–23
2022

M	T	W	T	F	S	S
				1	2
3	4	5	6	7	8	9
10	11	12	13	14	15	16
17	18	19	20	21	22	23
24	25	26	27	28	29	30
31

Upgrade Your Home Gym

Having a dedicated workout space makes enjoying a regular exercise routine so much easier. Here's what to keep in mind for the perfect setup.

LAY DOWN PADDED FLOORING. If you have the space, interlocking mat tiles can help protect the floor—and your knees! You can find an affordable set on Amazon and customize the size for your space.

BRIGHTEN UP THE ROOM. Turn walls into an uplifting focal point with bold colors, statement art or inspiring quotes that will encourage you to give 100% to your workout. Add a lamp or strip light, and consider a wall mount or holder to prop up your smartphone or tablet during virtual workouts.

STOCK A STURDY BASKET. Roll up your exercise mat post-workout and store it in a stylish woven storage hamper. Opt for one that stands up on its own and can fit a few rolled-up mats, a yoga block and workout bands.

ADD A FULL-LENGTH MIRROR. This not only helps make your space look bigger but also allows you to keep an eye on your form during complex exercise movements. If space is tight, hang one on the wall or behind a door.

17 MONDAY ○ Martin Luther King Jr. Day

18 TUESDAY

19 WEDNESDAY

20 THURSDAY

21 FRIDAY

22 SATURDAY

23 SUNDAY

JANUARY 24-30

2022

M	T	W	T	F	S	S
					1	2
3	4	5	6	7	8	9
10	11	12	13	14	15	16
17	18	19	20	21	22	23
24	25	26	27	28	29	30
31						

Beat Your Cravings

If your New Year's resolutions include getting a better handle on your diet, remember that you can't stress-eat junk that's not there.

CLEAR THE PANTRY. Rid the office snack stash of candy and treats when you know you're hitting a crazed period. Then stock up on no-effort crudités, air-popped popcorn and your favorite fruits. "I've never seen someone gain weight from simply eating too many pieces of fruit," says Wendy Bazilian, Dr.P.H., R.D.N.

SET AN ALARM. Remind yourself to take a break and eat something nutritious around 4 p.m. Avoid powering through work and then ravenously reaching for regret-it-later choices.

TAKE TIME TO ID THE TRIGGERS IN YOUR LIFE. To break the stress-eating cycle, seek out healthy ways to address them like taking a yoga class, opening a meditation app or taking a quick spin around the block when a big project goes haywire.

TRY THIS TO FEEL
··· CALM ···

If you dive into the candy dish, no biggie. **Give yourself a break** *— it happens! Get a good night's sleep and start fresh tomorrow.*

24 MONDAY

25 TUESDAY ◐

26 WEDNESDAY

27 THURSDAY

28 FRIDAY

29 SATURDAY

30 SUNDAY

FEBRUARY 2022

MONDAY	TUESDAY	WEDNESDAY	THURSDAY
	1 Chinese New Year ●	**2** Groundhog Day	**3**
7	**8** ◑	**9**	**10**
14 Valentine's Day	**15**	**16** ○	**17**
21 Presidents' Day	**22**	**23** ◐	**24**
28			

FRIDAY	SATURDAY	SUNDAY
4	5	6
11	12 Lincoln's Birthday	13
18	19	20
25	26	27

DON'T STRIVE FOR PERFECTION

Having self-love doesn't mean you never have another negative thought about yourself. When you're faced with a moment when your instinct is to beat yourself up, accept that inclination, but think about how you'd treat a loved one in the same situation.

This often makes it easier to **show compassion to yourself**, which opens the door to being able to work on forgiving yourself. Eventually, when you've learned to love who you see in the mirror, you'll rise to all kinds of challenges.

JANUARY

M	T	W	T	F	S	S
					1	2
3	4	5	6	7	8	9
10	11	12	13	14	15	16
17	18	19	20	21	22	23
24	25	26	27	28	29	30
31						

MARCH

M	T	W	T	F	S	S
	1	2	3	4	5	6
7	8	9	10	11	12	13
14	15	16	17	18	19	20
21	22	23	24	25	26	27
28	29	30	31			

JANUARY 31–FEBRUARY 6

2022

M	T	W	T	F	S	S
31	1	2	3	4	5	6
7	8	9	10	11	12	13
14	15	16	17	18	19	20
21	22	23	24	25	26	27
28						

"Love recognizes no barriers."

—MAYA ANGELOU

31 MONDAY

1 TUESDAY ● Chinese New Year

2 WEDNESDAY Groundhog Day

3 THURSDAY

4 FRIDAY

5 SATURDAY

6 SUNDAY

FEBRUARY 7-13
2022

M	T	W	T	F	S	S
	1	2	3	4	5	6
7	8	9	10	11	12	13
14	15	16	17	18	19	20
21	22	23	24	25	26	27
28						

Turn Nothing Into Something Inspiring

Having a vision of things that motivate you can help you envision important changes and goals you'd like to reach. Here's a great way to make an old crib spring into a graphic backdrop and an eye-catching spot to reflect your dreams.

STEP 1: PREP
Any scrap metal works wonders for this project as long as you start with a clean surface. Wipe down with a multisurface cleaner and lightly sand any chipped paint.

STEP 2: PAINT
Spray one or two coats of a gloss spray paint and let dry thoroughly. We like **Rust-Oleum** Gloss Protective Enamel Spray Paint.

STEP 3: DECORATE
Curate a meaningful collection of photos, images and found objects that inspire you, then secure with clothespins.

7 MONDAY

8 TUESDAY ◗

9 WEDNESDAY

10 THURSDAY

11 FRIDAY

12 SATURDAY Lincoln's Birthday

13 SUNDAY

FEBRUARY 14-20
2022

M	T	W	T	F	S	S
	1	2	3	4	5	6
7	8	9	10	11	12	13
14	15	16	17	18	19	20
21	22	23	24	25	26	27
28						

Make Sweet Treats Even Better

Decadent truffles usually contain heavy cream, but coconut milk is a wonderful substitute — fewer calories, same delicious richness.

VEGAN CHOCOLATE TRUFFLES

Active **25 min.** | Total **1 hr. 20 min.**

- **20** oz dark chocolate (72% cacao or higher), finely chopped and divided
- **⅓** cup coconut milk
- Toasted coconut flakes, optional

1. Place half of chocolate in a medium bowl. Heat coconut milk until hot to the touch, then pour over chocolate. Cover bowl loosely with a towel and let stand 5 min., then stir until melted and smooth.

2. Chill bowl until chocolate is firm enough to scoop but not rock hard, about 30 min. Scoop and roll tablespoon-size balls onto 1 piece of parchment paper; refrigerate.

3. Meanwhile, place remaining chocolate in a bowl; microwave on high in 30-sec. increments, stirring until melted and smooth.

4. Working 1 at a time, dip balls in chocolate, tapping off excess. Before chocolate has set, sprinkle with toasted coconut flakes if desired.

MAKES 30 TRUFFLES About 125 cal, 9.5 g fat (5.5 g sat), 2 g pro, 5 mg sodium, 9 g carb, 2 g fiber

14 MONDAY Valentine's Day

15 TUESDAY

16 WEDNESDAY ○

17 THURSDAY

18 FRIDAY

19 SATURDAY

20 SUNDAY

FEBRUARY 21–27
2022

M	T	W	T	F	S	S
	1	2	3	4	5	6
7	8	9	10	11	12	13
14	15	16	17	18	19	20
21	**22**	**23**	**24**	**25**	**26**	**27**
28						

Give Yourself a Massage

If there's no one else willing or able to work out the tension in your muscles, you can do it yourself. "There are sensory receptors in the skin that send messages to the brain, signaling that it's safe to relax," says Kiera Nagle, M.A., L.M.T., C.P.M.T., director of massage programs at Pacific College of Health and Science. It also makes you more aware of where you're feeling tense so you can consciously relax those areas of your body, she adds. Some good spots you can reach yourself are the muscles of your shoulders, the hinge of your jaw and pressure points on your hands.

TRY THIS TO FEEL
••• CALM •••

*When you can feel your stress level rising, do this **30-second stretch to reset:** Close your eyes, drop your shoulders, and roll your head around. (Need a time-out reminder? Cue yourself to do this any time you hear a phone ring, a car honk or any other sonic signal.)*

21 MONDAY Presidents' Day

22 TUESDAY

23 WEDNESDAY ☽

24 THURSDAY

25 FRIDAY

26 SATURDAY

27 SUNDAY

MARCH 2022

MONDAY	TUESDAY	WEDNESDAY	THURSDAY
	1	2 ●	3
7	8	9	10 ◐
14 Pi Day	15	16	17 St. Patrick's Day Holi Begins
21	22	23	24
28	29	30	31

FRIDAY	SATURDAY	SUNDAY
4	**5**	**6**
11	**12**	**13** Daylight Savings Time Begins
18 ○	**19**	**20** First Day of Spring
25 ◑	**26**	**27**

Feel Good Goal

GET THE SLEEP YOU DESERVE

Just one night of spotty sleep can leave you with a number of unpleasant effects the next day—irritability, lack of focus, reduced vigilance, higher risk of accidents and fatigue. To get seven to eight hours of restful sleep, **try blocking all the light**.

There's some evidence that light can penetrate eyelids and interfere with melatonin production. Even illumination from streetlights, a clock, the cable box or under the door may have an effect, so it's worth installing blackout curtains and slipping on an eye mask.

FEBRUARY

M	T	W	T	F	S	S
	1	2	3	4	5	6
7	8	9	10	11	12	13
14	15	16	17	18	19	20
21	22	23	24	25	26	27
28						

APRIL

M	T	W	T	F	S	S
				1	2	3
4	5	6	7	8	9	10
11	12	13	14	15	16	17
18	19	20	21	22	23	24
25	26	27	28	29	30	

FEBRUARY 28–
MARCH 6

2022

M	T	W	T	F	S	S
28	1	2	3	4	5	6
7	8	9	10	11	12	13
14	15	16	17	18	19	20
21	22	23	24	25	26	27
28	29	30	31			

"Sleep is the best meditation."

—DALAI LAMA

28 MONDAY

1 TUESDAY

2 WEDNESDAY ●

3 THURSDAY

4 FRIDAY

5 SATURDAY

6 SUNDAY

MARCH 7-13

2022

M	T	W	T	F	S	S
	1	2	3	4	5	6
7	8	9	10	11	12	13
14	15	16	17	18	19	20
21	22	23	24	25	26	27
28	29	30	31			

Boost Your Beautifying Rest

Anything that keeps you up at night can stand between you and glowing skin. "Sleep is when your skin cells repair themselves and regenerate," says Melanie Palm, M.D., a dermatologist in San Diego. "If that period is shortened or altered, skin cells can't perform at their optimum level."

Solid rest contributes to lusher hair too. "Sleep is necessary for proper protein synthesis in the production of hair strands as well," explains Whitney Bowe, M.D., a New York dermatologist and the author of *Dirty Looks: The Secret to Beautiful Skin*. So aim to log about seven to eight hours of sleep per night and . . .

FOR ADDED ANTI-AGING BENEFITS

Apply a night treatment with an ingredient like retinol to boost collagen production while you doze. To maximize moisturizing power, swap in an extra-nourishing overnight mask weekly in place of night cream.

TO GET SOFTER, HEALTHIER HAIR

Try smoothing a no-residue deep conditioner meant to be worn overnight all over damp or dry strands before bed once or twice per week.

7 MONDAY

8 TUESDAY

9 WEDNESDAY

10 THURSDAY ◑

11 FRIDAY

12 SATURDAY

13 SUNDAY Daylight Savings Time Begins

MARCH 14-20
2022

M	T	W	T	F	S	S
	1	2	3	4	5	6
7	8	9	10	11	12	13
14	**15**	**16**	**17**	**18**	**19**	**20**
21	22	23	24	25	26	27
28	29	30	31			

Savor a Sleep-Inducing Smoothie

Tart cherry juice is a potent source of melatonin, which helps ease you into restful slumber. In a blender, combine ¾ cup of **Montmorency (tart) cherry juice**, 1 cup of **fat-free vanilla Greek yogurt**, and 1 cup of **ice cubes.** Blend on high to desired consistency.

MORE PRE-SNOOZE SNACKS

Looking for more options? Jaclyn London, M.S., R.D., C.D.N., head of nutrition and wellness at WW, suggests the following:

PISTACHIOS These are packed with protein, vitamin B6 and magnesium, all of which contribute to better sleep. "Don't exceed a 1-ounce portion of nuts," London warns. "Anything too high in calories can have the reverse effect of keeping you awake!"

PRUNES The nutrients in dried plums—vitamin B6, calcium and magnesium—produce melatonin. Top whole-grain toast with prunes or eat them on their own about 30 minutes before bedtime.

HERBAL TEA A cup of herbal tea has tons of snooze-promoting properties. "Chamomile tea is excellent for calming nerves before bedtime," says London.

14 MONDAY Pi Day

15 TUESDAY

16 WEDNESDAY

17 THURSDAY St. Patrick's Day
Holi Begins

18 FRIDAY ○

19 SATURDAY

20 SUNDAY First Day of Spring

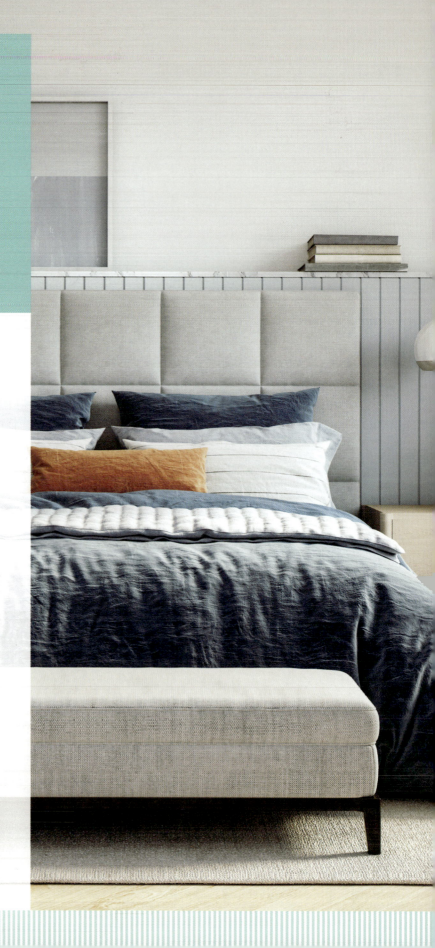

MARCH 21-27
2022

M	T	W	T	F	S	S
28	1	2	3	4	5	6
7	8	9	10	11	12	13
14	15	16	17	18	19	20
21	22	23	24	25	26	27
28	29	30	31			

Pick the Perfect-for-You Mattress

THINK ABOUT WHERE TO BUY. Shop in-store if you want a greater variety and to feel them before buying. You can also negotiate the price. Buy online if you have trouble making decisions, since there are fewer options. Plus, you can shop from home.

FIND YOUR FIRMNESS. Traditional innerspring styles have that familiar bouncy feel and may be firmer. Memory foam options have less spring and offer more pressure relief. In general, side sleepers need a softer mattress, stomach sleepers need a firm one and back sleepers fall somewhere in between.

ASK ABOUT THE RETURN POLICY. You may get a partial refund if you bought it in a store, but online companies often arrange to pick it up for a local charity and will give back 100% of your money. Make sure you can test out a new mattress for a month risk-free so you can get used to it before making a decision.

TRY THIS TO FEEL
···• CALM •···

*Once you're physically in bed, try a mental exercise to quiet your mind. **Imagine a relaxing scene** — its soothing sights, smells and sounds — until you fall asleep.*

21 MONDAY

22 TUESDAY

23 WEDNESDAY

24 THURSDAY

25 FRIDAY

26 SATURDAY

27 SUNDAY

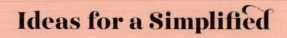

Ideas for a Simplified
SPRING

Ditch the clutter with easy ways to organize
and focus on what matters most.

KEEP ONLY
What You Love

It can be difficult to let go of certain items that hold a special significance, but minimizing the clutter opens the door to new possibilities. Let these three benefits of minimizing inspire you to start tossing:

AN OPPORTUNITY TO FOCUS
When you walk into a room without a lot of visual distractions, bright pops of color are more pronounced.

CLEANER SURFACES If you have to constantly move things around to clean them, you're not only creating more work for yourself, you're also less likely to be successful. This fact applies to furniture as well as flooring, so make a thorough sweep of those piles once and for all.

EFFICIENCY It may seem obvious, but here's a truth that bears repeating. Once you have a clutter-management routine that works, finding everything becomes far easier.

Make Your Kitchen Feel Twice as Big

A WELL-ORGANIZED PANTRY is a game changer for any home chef. As you know, it's all too easy for the pantry to become an out-of-sight, out-of-mind catchall for half-empty containers, spare plastic bags and more unnecessary clutter. But once you get your shelves in order, cooking weeknight dinners, putting away groceries and packing snacks for school lunches can finally be as easy as opening the pantry door. Best of all: Most of these clever tips and tricks can work in the rest of your kitchen so you can keep the organized flow going.

ARRANGE BASKETS HIGH AND LOW.

Whether your pantry is out in the open or closed off in a room, take advantage of vertical wall space by scattering baskets on high and low shelves. Place seasonal items in the baskets up high (Christmas cookie cutters, for example) and kid-friendly essentials down below.

KEEP BAKING SUPPLIES WITHIN REACH.

Transfer common ingredients— flour, sugar, brown sugar, pasta and so on—into large glass jars with lids and place them on the middle shelf for easy access. On the shelf above, arrange small glass jars full of more specialized ingredients, like spices, nuts and dried fruit.

ADD DECALS TO JARS.

Keep track of what's what with cute, decorative decals marking flour, sugar and more. Pro tip: Use a dry erase marker to write down the expiration date before you decant it into the container.

LABEL EVERYTHING.

Set yourself up for success by giving every basket, container and bin an easy-to-read, interchangeable label. Same goes for your trash and recycling bins.

TURN PANTRY DOORS INTO CHALKBOARDS.

Make the pantry doors more functional with chalkboard paint or contact paper so you can write down grocery lists, important reminders and sweet notes to your family members.

TAKE CANS AND JARS OFF THE SHELVES. For those items you can't transfer into a different container, find a way to keep them better organized. When you arrange them by category—fruits, veggies, sauces and more—in a pull-out wire shelf, you can find exactly what you need without the hassle.

Hat Trick

Create this easy DIY organizer that doubles as decor and doesn't require putting multiple holes in your wall, suggests Sabrina Tan, founder of fashion and lifestyle blog *Gypsy Tan* (@gypsytan). All you need are a copper pipe, clothesline rope, clothespins and one nail.

CLEAR CLOSET CLUTTER FOR GOOD

Here's a valuable lesson for streamlining a closet: Deciding what to keep in your wardrobe is only half the battle. Choosing how to keep it all organized neatly is just as important.

ORGANIZE BY CATEGORY AND ACTIVITY.
Even if you don't have an extensive pants collection, you'll still save major time in the morning if you organize your clothing by type of item—not color—and keep similar garments grouped together. Along the same lines, use bins or drawers to keep workout gear and comfortable weekend wear in their own place, separate from dress clothes.

COLOR-COORDINATE YOUR CONTAINERS.
The easiest way to take your closet from junky to jaw-dropping? Pick your colors wisely: All-white hangers look super clean, while light blue containers add an element of surprise.

USE EVERY NOOK AND CRANNY.
Fill open shelves with bins, jewelry organizers and labeled baskets. You can even add smaller fabric bins below rods full of clothes to store belts and other accessories.

DON'T FORGET THE SPACE UP TOP.
Savvy storage boxes with handles are basically made for keeping out-of-season clothes stacked above your clothing rod. The higher you go, the more space you can add (just don't forget to invest in a safe step stool).

LABEL LIKE CRAZY.
The more you take advantage of labels, the less likely you'll end up throwing that random sock without a mate into whatever bin you come across (and then losing it in the black hole that is your closet forever).

APRIL 2022

MONDAY	TUESDAY	WEDNESDAY	THURSDAY
4	5	6	7
11	12	13	14
18	19	20	21
25	26	27	28

FRIDAY	SATURDAY	SUNDAY
1 April Fools' Day ●	**2** Ramadan Begins	**3**
8	**9** ◑	**10** Palm Sunday
15 Passover Begins Tax Day	**16** ○	**17** Easter Sunday
22 Earth Day	**23** ◐	**24**
29 Arbor Day Lailat al-Qadr	**30** ●	

Feel Good Goal

BE GREENER

Want to help the environment but not sure where to begin? There are plenty of ways to make a difference. And **little changes can have a big impact**. Don't let yourself get overwhelmed thinking you have to overhaul everything at once. Just pick a few ideas—maybe aim to consolidate orders to minimize shipping, swap out disposables for reusables or use a refill station for water—and see how they work. Over time, you can reduce your household's impact on the environment considerably.

MARCH

M	T	W	T	F	S	S
	1	2	3	4	5	6
7	8	9	10	11	12	13
14	15	16	17	18	19	20
21	22	23	24	25	26	27
28	29	30	31			

MAY

M	T	W	T	F	S	S
						1
2	3	4	5	6	7	8
9	10	11	12	13	14	15
16	17	18	19	20	21	22
23	24	25	26	27	28	29
30	31					

MARCH 28–APRIL 3

2022

M	T	W	T	F	S	S
28	29	30	31	1	2	3
4	5	6	7	8	9	10
11	12	13	14	15	16	17
18	19	20	21	22	23	24
25	26	27	28	29	30	

"Real generosity toward the future lies in giving all to the present."

— ALBERT CAMUS

28 MONDAY

29 TUESDAY

30 WEDNESDAY

31 THURSDAY

1 FRIDAY ● April Fools' Day

2 SATURDAY Ramadan Begins

3 SUNDAY

M	T	W	T	F	S	S
				1	2	3
4	5	6	7	8	9	10
11	12	13	14	15	16	17
18	19	20	21	22	23	24
25	26	27	28	29	30	

Feed Your Plants, Save the Planet

Around 30% of what we throw away is food scraps and yard waste. If you're on the fence about starting your own compost pile, here's what may convince you to get started. You can compost most everything into (free!) plant food:

KITCHEN SCRAPS: Almost anything from your kitchen and garden can go into the bin, including eggshells, cut flowers, coffee grounds (and paper filters), old newspapers, tea and tea bags, hair, toothpicks and matches.

GREEN WASTE: Fruit and veggie scraps, grass clippings and coffee or tea leaves supply compost with nitrogen, key for healthy soil.

BROWN WASTE: Wood shavings or ash, dry leaves or paper shopping bags are rich in carbon, which helps break down the other scraps. A balance of both green and brown waste is important.

WHAT TO AVOID: Dairy or animal products will cause compost to smell and attract pests, so toss those in your old-school garbage can. The same goes for fats, oils and pet waste. Keep it balanced.

4 MONDAY

5 TUESDAY

6 WEDNESDAY

7 THURSDAY

8 FRIDAY

9 SATURDAY ☽

10 SUNDAY Palm Sunday

M	T	W	T	F	S	S
				1	2	3
4	5	6	7	8	9	10
11	12	13	14	15	16	17
18	19	20	21	22	23	24
25	26	27	28	29	30	

Get Crafty With Upcycled Gifts

Need a quick hostess gift on the fly? Consider one of these easy projects for a heartfelt offering.

WRAP CANS IN PRETTY PAPER — INSTANT VASES! Rinse each can clean and file down sharp edges, then measure its height. Cut wrapping paper or wallpaper to fit before securing with double-stick tape.

CREATE ROCKIN' BOTTLE STOPPERS. Save the wine corks from your next dinner party and turn them into the perfect hostess gift with a little hot glue and a few gems. Etsy is a great source for affordable bling.

PLACE SUCCULENTS IN A BRICK PLANTER. Scoop potting soil into a holey brick and pop in a few small succulents. Use bricks from a leftover home project or buy them at your hardware store.

TRY THIS TO FEEL
•••• CALM ••••
Not up for a craft project?
*Just **draw a simple doodle** and*
let your mind wander.

11 MONDAY

12 TUESDAY

13 WEDNESDAY

14 THURSDAY

15 FRIDAY Passover Begins
Tax Day

16 SATURDAY ○

17 SUNDAY Easter Sunday

APRIL 18-24
2022

M	T	W	T	F	S	S
				1	2	3
4	5	6	7	8	9	10
11	12	13	14	15	16	17
18	19	20	21	22	23	24
25	26	27	28	29	30	

Enjoy the Taste of Spring

Skip the lettuce and use a mandoline to cut veggies super thin to give your salad a delicious, delicate crunch.

CARROT-RADISH SALAD

Active **25 min.** | Total **25 min.**

- 3 Tbsp fresh orange juice
- 3 Tbsp fresh lemon juice
- 1 tsp honey
- ½ tsp each kosher salt and pepper
- 3 Tbsp olive oil
- 4 mixed-colored carrots, shaved lengthwise (about 3 cups)
- 4 radishes, shaved into rounds (about 1 cup)
- 2 stalks celery, thinly sliced (about 2 cups)
- 1 small beet, shaved into half moons (about 1 cup)
- 1 cup watercress
- 2 small oranges, rind removed and sliced into half moons
- ½ cup fresh mint leaves, torn if large

1. In a bowl whisk together orange juice, lemon juice, honey, and salt and pepper to dissolve the honey then whisk in olive oil. Set aside.

2. On a platter, arrange carrots, radishes, celery, beet, watercress, oranges and mint leaves. Drizzle with vinaigrette.

SERVES 6 About 115 cal, 7 g fat (1 g sat), 2 g pro, 235 mg sodium, 13 g carb, 3 g fiber

18 MONDAY

19 TUESDAY

20 WEDNESDAY

21 THURSDAY

22 FRIDAY Earth Day

23 SATURDAY ○

24 SUNDAY

MAY 2022

MONDAY	TUESDAY	WEDNESDAY	THURSDAY
2 May Day Eid al-Fitr	**3**	**4**	**5** Cinco de Mayo
9	**10**	**11**	**12**
16 ○	**17**	**18**	**19**
23	**24**	**25**	**26**
30 Memorial Day ●	**31**		

FRIDAY	SATURDAY	SUNDAY
		1
6	**7**	**8** Mother's Day ◖
13	**14**	**15**
20	**21** Armed Forces Day	**22** ◗
27	**28**	**29**

MAKE YOUR HOUSE A HAVEN

No matter how clean you keep your house, there are tons of odors that will develop naturally. **Whip up a DIY home fragrance** by looking to your spice rack, fruit bowl or herb garden for a clean, fresh scent that won't irritate sensitive noses.

- Simmer citrus peels and cinnamon in water on the stove.
- Bring in the pleasant smell of the outdoors with plants like jasmine and gardenias.
- Arrange fresh herbs (mint, rosemary, lavender) in vases.

APRIL

M	T	W	T	F	S	S
				1	2	3
4	5	6	7	8	9	10
11	12	13	14	15	16	17
18	19	20	21	22	23	24
25	26	27	28	29	30	

JUNE

M	T	W	T	F	S	S
		1	2	3	4	5
6	7	8	9	10	11	12
13	14	15	16	17	18	19
20	21	22	23	24	25	26
27	28	29	30			

APRIL 25–MAY 1

2022

M	T	W	T	F	S	S
25	**26**	**27**	**28**	**29**	**30**	**1**
2	3	4	5	6	7	8
9	10	11	12	13	14	15
16	17	18	19	20	21	22
23	24	25	26	27	28	29
30	31					

"Home is the nicest word there is."

— LAURA INGALLS WILDER

25 MONDAY ○

26 TUESDAY

27 WEDNESDAY

28 THURSDAY

29 FRIDAY Arbor Day
Lailat al-Qadr

30 SATURDAY ●

1 SUNDAY

M	T	W	T	F	S	S
						1
2	3	4	5	6	7	8
9	10	11	12	13	14	15
16	17	18	19	20	21	22
23	24	25	26	27	28	29
30	31					

Create an Office Hideaway

You don't need the luxury of an extra room to carve out a dedicated work space. Take a cue from Instagram influencer Allison Freeman of @theclevergoose, who transformed her guest room's closet into an office by adding a desktop and a few shelves. Ready for the weekend? Push in the chair, shut the door, and your work space disappears. "Since the office lives behind a door, no one has to be reminded of work when it's not in use, like when guests are visiting or we're watching TV," she says.

TRY THIS TO FEEL
···· CALM ····

*Finding it difficult to concentrate on work? Close your eyes and **focus on your breathing**. Let your mind slow down as you silently count to 5 with each inhale and exhale.*

2 **MONDAY** May Day
Eid al-Fitr

3 **TUESDAY**

4 **WEDNESDAY**

5 **THURSDAY** Cinco de Mayo

6 **FRIDAY**

7 **SATURDAY**

8 **SUNDAY** ☽ Mother's Day

MAY 9-15

2022

M	T	W	T	F	S	S
						1
2	3	4	5	6	7	8
9	10	11	12	13	14	15
16	17	18	19	20	21	22
23	24	25	26	27	28	29
30	31					

Make Personalized Portraits

Silhouette art, which became popular in the 18th century, can add a personal touch to any modern decor. It's a timeless and relatively easy way to create a customized keepsake of loved ones without having to take a drawing class.

You can send a side-profile photo to an online art retailer like Minted.com, which created the art featured here, or use this simple how-to from Dallas-based interior designer Courtney Warren to create your own.

1. Position your subject perpendicular to a blank wall and snap a photo in profile.

2. Add a black-and-white filter to the picture and print it out at 4" x 6" or 5" x 7". Then glue the image onto black card stock and cut out the silhouette.

3. Flip it over and place it in a frame on a white mat or patterned paper.

LILY BELLE

9 MONDAY

10 TUESDAY

11 WEDNESDAY

12 THURSDAY

13 FRIDAY

14 SATURDAY

15 SUNDAY

MAY 16-22
2022

M	T	W	T	F	S	S
						1
2	3	4	5	6	7	8
9	10	11	12	13	14	15
16	**17**	**18**	**19**	**20**	**21**	**22**
23	24	25	26	27	28	29
30	31					

Have a Nighttime Tidy-Up Routine

Make these touch-ups before bedtime, and you'll never wake up to a morning mess again.

VACUUM THE FLOOR. Go under and around the table with a rechargeable stick vacuum like the Bissell Adapt Ion XRT 2-in-1 Cordless Vacuum. It's got an onboard hand vac, and the handle folds down for compact storage.

SANITIZE THE COUNTERTOPS. Wipe up spills and gather crumbs, then spritz these surfaces with a fast-acting sanitizing multipurpose cleaner like GH Seal star Microban 24 Hour. It kills germs in just 60 seconds and gives you 24-hour protection.

WIPE THE COOKTOP. Rinse a cloth or a sponge in hot water and wipe any splatters around burners, in drip pans or on glass.

NEATEN THE SINK. Load the dishwasher and, if needed, hand-wash and dry any stray items. Stash tools and cleaners under the sink or neatly in caddies. Buff the faucet dry.

TIDY THE TRASH. Make sure all the trash is inside the can and that recyclables are contained or taken out. Wipe down the can with an antibacterial wipe if you see drips.

16 MONDAY ○

17 TUESDAY

18 WEDNESDAY

19 THURSDAY

20 FRIDAY

21 SATURDAY Armed Forces Day

22 ◑ SUNDAY

M	T	W	T	F	S	S
						1
2	3	4	5	6	7	8
9	10	11	12	13	14	15
16	17	18	19	20	21	22
23	24	25	26	27	28	29
30	31					

Ready, Set, Play!

If you'd like to generate some more productive family bonding, consider adopting a monthly game night. These bonus benefits will last long after the winner is called.

BUILD SOCIAL AND COGNITIVE SKILLS. Games "teach children to work as a team, negotiate, follow rules and use spatial reasoning and logic," explains Ellie Dix, a former school behavior specialist and author of *The Board Game Family: Reclaim Your Children From the Screen.*

IMPROVE KIDS' RESPONSE TO DELAYED GRATIFICATION. Many digital games provide a quick hit of the "happy chemicals" dopamine and oxytocin, which is why they're so addictive, says Hanna Bogen Novak, M.S., a director at the Center for Connection family therapy practice. Board games are a slower burn, and regular play can retrain brains to get the same buzz from a delayed release of chemicals. That helps kids focus on long-term projects like schoolwork too.

23 MONDAY

24 TUESDAY

25 WEDNESDAY

26 THURSDAY

27 FRIDAY

28 SATURDAY

29 SUNDAY

JUNE 2022

MONDAY	TUESDAY	WEDNESDAY	THURSDAY
		1	**2**
6	**7** ◑	**8**	**9**
13	**14** Flag Day ○	**15**	**16**
20 ◐	**21** First Day of Summer	**22**	**23**
27	**28** ●	**29**	**30**

FRIDAY	SATURDAY	SUNDAY
3	**4**	**5**
10	**11**	**12**
17	**18**	**19** Father's Day Juneteenth
24	**25**	**26**

FIND YOUR FOCUS

Aim your brain at a problem. If you feel as if your mind is looping around itself, give yourself a task such as organizing your shoes or doing a word puzzle. When you're stressed, your brain may be saying, *Let's solve this problem!* — so it keeps spinning, but that's actually a good time to engage your mind. If you **give your brain a short-term task** to focus on, you'll feel calmer and be better able to deal with what's actually bothering you.

MAY						
M	**T**	**W**	**T**	**F**	**S**	**S**
						1
2	3	4	5	6	7	8
9	10	11	12	13	14	15
16	17	18	19	20	21	22
23	24	25	26	27	28	29
30	31					

JULY						
M	**T**	**W**	**T**	**F**	**S**	**S**
				1	2	3
4	5	6	7	8	9	10
11	12	13	14	15	16	17
18	19	20	21	22	23	24
25	26	27	28	29	30	31

M	T	W	T	F	S	S
30	31	1	2	3	4	5
6	7	8	9	10	11	12
13	14	15	16	17	18	19
20	21	22	23	24	25	26
27	28	29	30			

"Freedom lies in being bold."

— ROBERT FROST

30 **MONDAY** ● Memorial Day

31 **TUESDAY**

1 **WEDNESDAY**

2 **THURSDAY**

3 **FRIDAY**

4 **SATURDAY**

5 **SUNDAY**

JUNE 6-12
2022

M	T	W	T	F	S	S
			1	2	3	4	5
6	7	8	9	10	11	12
13	14	15	16	17	18	19
20	21	22	23	24	25	26
27	28	29	30			

Sprinkle On Brain-Boosting Spice!

The main compound in curry—turmeric—has been linked to major protective benefits against cognitive decline. In fact, research published in *Stem Cell Research & Therapy* showed that individuals who consumed curry even just about once a month still performed better on standardized tests than those who rarely or never ate curry. Need more proof? Older adults in India are much less likely (4.4 times less as of 2008) to develop Alzheimer's than those in the United States.

While there are plenty of delicious curry dishes out there, you don't need complex recipes to enjoy the benefits of curry powder. Try:

- Sprinkling it on top of popcorn
- Adding a dash to deviled eggs
- Mixing it into chicken salad

TRY THIS TO FEEL
···· CALM ····

Take an extra moment to rinse your hands under warm running water. Imagine your stress leaving your fingers and going down the drain.

6 MONDAY

7 TUESDAY ☽

8 WEDNESDAY

9 THURSDAY

10 FRIDAY

11 SATURDAY

12 SUNDAY

JUNE 13-19
2022

M	T	W	T	F	S	S
		1	2	3	4	5
6	7	8	9	10	11	12
13	**14**	**15**	**16**	**17**	**18**	**19**
20	21	22	23	24	25	26
27	28	29	30			

Talk Yourself Resilient

Roughly 40% of our overall happiness is thought to derive not from our circumstances or genes but from our own actions. Reframing negative self-talk (catastrophizing, self-blame, blaming others and defeatist thinking) is one technique that can help bring out the strong, confident woman you have inside. Here are some examples to consider.

INSTEAD OF: "I NEVER GET THE BEST ASSIGNMENTS AT WORK. MY BOSS MUST THINK I'M AN IDIOT."
TRY: "My boss doesn't yet know what I'm capable of. I'll come up with a list of new projects I'd love to tackle, and that will help her see me in a new light."

INSTEAD OF: "MY HOUSE WILL NEVER LOOK AS STYLISH AS MY NEIGHBOR'S. WHY EVEN BOTHER?"
TRY: "We put our savings into a college fund rather than spending it on expensive furniture. That was a smart choice for us, and we love our comfortably messy den!"

INSTEAD OF: "I BROUGHT THIS BREAKUP ON MYSELF — I ALWAYS PICK LOSERS WHO CAN'T COMMIT."
TRY: "Blaming myself or my ex won't make me feel better. What did I learn from this relationship that will help me find a more compatible partner next time?"

13 MONDAY

14 TUESDAY ○ Flag Day

15 WEDNESDAY

16 THURSDAY

17 FRIDAY

18 SATURDAY

19 SUNDAY Father's Day
Juneteenth

JUNE 20-26
2022

M	T	W	T	F	S	S
		1	2	3	4	5
6	7	8	9	10	11	12
13	14	15	16	17	18	19
20	**21**	**22**	**23**	**24**	**25**	**26**
27	28	29	30			

Plan a Play Date for You and Your Friends

Researchers aren't sure why, but having a strong social life seems to be protective against cognitive decline. In fact, studies have found that people with more positive social relationships than their peers have better brainpower as they age. So go ahead and do a girls' night in with margaritas and a movie.

BLOOD ORANGE MARGARITAS

Active **10 min.** | Total **10 min.**

Kosher salt
Crushed ice
½ cup fresh blood orange juice
2 oz tequila
1 oz triple sec or Cointreau
Orange wedges (optional)

Moisten rim of 2 margarita glasses and dip in **kosher salt**. Fill a cocktail shaker with **crushed ice**. Add **fresh blood orange juice**, **tequila**, and **triple sec** or **Cointreau**. Shake well and strain into glasses. Garnish with **orange wedges** if desired.

20 MONDAY ◑

21 TUESDAY First Day of Summer

22 WEDNESDAY

23 THURSDAY

24 FRIDAY

25 SATURDAY

26 SUNDAY

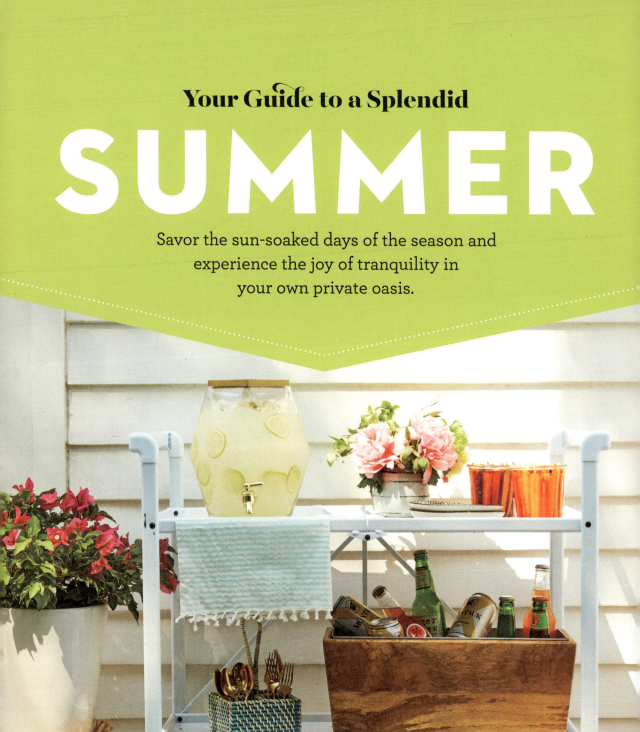

Your Guide to a Splendid

SUMMER

Savor the sun-soaked days of the season and
experience the joy of tranquility in
your own private oasis.

SIMPLE DECORATING IDEAS FOR
Instant Relaxation

SWING INTO SUMMER. A rattan or wicker hanging chair adds a fun touch to just about any space and brings a bit of the outdoors in. Place one in the corner of a bedroom, use it to add charm to your reading nook or let your kids sway away in the playroom. To install a hammock chair, simply drill hardware into a ceiling stud.

MAKE A HANDY BAR CART. Turn a simple bar cart into a conversation starter that's ideal for entertaining. Rest a beverage dispenser on a patterned towel, add a gorgeous bouquet and use decorative containers for drinks and bar tools.

ROLL OUT A PATIO CARPET. A simple waterproof area rug instantly makes any outdoor space feel cozier—and helps create the feeling of a room.

Maximize a Small Garden

Regardless of the size of your outdoor space, you'll need to figure out its sun and wind exposure before heading to the garden center, advises Penn State Extension master gardener Nancy Knauss. Then choose plants ideal for that environment, keeping size in mind. Compact shrubs won't need constant pruning, climbing plants grow up instead of out and containers give you big bang for the buck.

Also, think about how much time you have to devote to your plants. Hanging baskets and small planters may need daily watering, as there's not much soil in them. Even if you're working with a tiny porch or a pocket-size yard, you can still craft your very own private oasis. Brighten up a small space with some of these creative garden tips.

PLANT PALLET
Use steel ties and nails to anchor small pots to a recycled pallet for a vertical herb bed.

FAIRY GARDEN
Craft some whimsy in a pot. Small plants, pebbles and doll furniture create pint-size magic.

SUCCULENT BATH
Add personality with unexpected planters. Try using a birdbath for shallow-soil succulents.

VINE FENCE
Climbing plants create a natural privacy screen that makes your garden look bigger.

GET YOUR GARAGE & SHED IN ORDER

DISPLAY TOOLS. Rather than leaning lawn essentials against the wall, keep shovels, rakes, pruning shears and other garden go-tos within reach by mounting them on a pegboard panel. Even big items like hoses and wheelbarrows can be roped up with strong bungee cords.

REPURPOSE HOME BASICS. Creativity can give old kitchen organizers fresh life. A magnetic knife strip is great to corral small items and keep them contained but easy to find. Old film canisters, mini mason jars and pillboxes can be new homes for nuts, bolts and nails: Label them and tuck them neatly away in long horizontal spice trays to tidy up your active workspace.

SEE YOUR STUFF. Limit rummaging by stowing similar items in opaque lidded bins. Extension cords, rags and other bulky items can live in wire baskets for visibility.

USE EVERY INCH OF SPACE. Tuck bikes and sports equipment below wall-mounted shelves or suspend them from a garage ceiling so they won't hog square footage. Install rails to free up precious counter space and hang frequently used items in baskets, on hooks or inside tool holders.

GET READY FOR A BACKYARD PARTY

Looking for a quick way to add festive flair to your outdoor event? These simple ideas can be accomplished in an afternoon:

BUILD A FIRE PIT. Construct a fire pit by arranging curved paving stones in a circle. It's tip-proof, even without mortar, and the entire undertaking takes just 20 minutes from start to finish.

FLOAT A FLOWER ARRANGEMENT. Before guests come over, pop some floating candles and zinnias in a birdbath for an instant water feature.

CUT BANDANNAS INTO SWAGS. All you need to do is cut a square bandanna into a triangle and hot-glue it onto some twine. Pick any color you like and repeat until you get the perfect length.

Take Dessert Outside

SPICED GRILLED PINEAPPLE

Active **5 min.** | Total **10 min.**

Juicy pineapple dipped in coconut sugar and cinnamon, then grilled until golden and caramelized, is the perfect summer dessert. A sprinkle of lime zest is highly recommended, a scoop of vanilla ice cream is nonnegotiable.

HOW TO BUY THE BEST PINEAPPLE

Look for a pineapple that is firm but not hard, with a deep yellow-orange tone. Pay attention to the smell and sound of the fruit — if ripe, it shouldn't smell sickly sweet or have a hollow sound. Store whole pineapple right on the counter if you plan to eat it in the next 1 to 3 days. To prolong shelf life, store in the refrigerator for up to 5 days.

3 Tbsp coconut sugar
2 tsp ground cinnamon
1 tsp ground cardamom
1 medium pineapple, rind removed, cut into ½-in.-thick rounds (about 8 slices total)
Vanilla ice cream and grated lime zest, for serving

1. Heat grill to medium-low.
2. In shallow bowl, mix together coconut sugar, cinnamon and cardamom.
3. Sprinkle each side of pineapple slices with coconut sugar mixture (about ½ tsp per side), rubbing mixture into pineapple. Grill until deep golden brown and caramelized, 3 to 4 min. per side.
4. Transfer to plates or platter. Serve with vanilla ice cream and sprinkle with lime zest if desired.

SERVES 6 About 105 cal, 0.5 g fat (0 g sat), 1 g pro, 5 mg sodium, 28 g carb, 1 g fiber

Flavor Booster!
Use coconut ice cream instead of vanilla for a tropical (and dairy-free) twist.

JULY 2022

MONDAY	TUESDAY	WEDNESDAY	THURSDAY
4 Independence Day	**5**	**6** ◐	**7**
11	**12**	**13** ○	**14**
18	**19**	**20** ◑	**21**
25	**26**	**27**	**28** ●

FRIDAY	SATURDAY	SUNDAY
1	2	3
8	9	10
15	16	17
22	23	24
29	30	31

CELEBRATE WHAT YOU LOVE

Acknowledge who you are and **have your living space reflect the real you.** "If something isn't adding beauty to your life right now, you don't need to keep it," says professional organizer Jeni Aron. Some inspirational ideas on what to toss:

- Embrace your body by purging clothes that don't fit.
- Embrace your career by tossing paperwork that no longer matters.
- Embrace your current relationship by getting rid of unwanted items from former relationships.

JUNE

M	T	W	T	F	S	S
		1	2	3	4	5
6	7	8	9	10	11	12
13	14	15	16	17	18	19
20	21	22	23	24	25	26
27	28	29	30			

AUGUST

M	T	W	T	F	S	S
1	2	3	4	5	6	7
8	9	10	11	12	13	14
15	16	17	18	19	20	21
22	23	24	25	26	27	28
29	30	31				

M	T	W	T	F	S	S
27	28	29	30	1	2	3
4	5	6	7	8	9	10
11	12	13	14	15	16	17
18	19	20	21	22	23	24
25	26	27	28	29	30	31

"Patriotism is like charity—it begins at home."

—HENRY JAMES

27 MONDAY

28 TUESDAY ●

29 WEDNESDAY

30 THURSDAY

1 FRIDAY

2 SATURDAY

3 SUNDAY

JULY 4-10
2022

M	T	W	T	F	S	S
				1	2	3
4	5	6	7	8	9	10
11	12	13	14	15	16	17
18	19	20	21	22	23	24
25	26	27	28	29	30	31

Try These Tasty Toppers

Whether you're grilling up burgers, chicken, steak or fish for a sandwich, pile on one of these colorful combos for a memorable holiday feast.

DECONSTRUCTED GUAC Diced Avocado + Lime Juice + Cilantro + Queso Fresco

LOUISIANA'S FAVORITE Sliced Tomato + Grilled Red Onion + Cajun Seasoning

GREEN MONSTER Granny Smith Apple + Watercress + Grilled Scallion

TRY THIS TO FEEL
••• CALM •••

*Keeping your menu super simple is a great strategy for avoiding party meltdowns. Another is **using your grill to its full potential**. While the meats are getting a good sear, wrap potatoes in foil and put right on the fire. You can also grill fruit directly on the grate.*

4 MONDAY Independence Day

5 TUESDAY

6 WEDNESDAY ◑

7 THURSDAY

8 FRIDAY

9 SATURDAY

10 SUNDAY

JULY 11-17
2022

M	T	W	T	F	S	S
				1	2	3
4	5	6	7	8	9	10
11	12	13	14	15	16	17
18	19	20	21	22	23	24
25	26	27	28	29	30	31

Beat a Headache Naturally

Summer is a dreadful time to get bogged down with headache pain, especially when there are so many other things you'd rather be doing. But before you pop a pill, try one of these strategies instead:

PUT DOWN YOUR PHONE. Light and noise often make migraines worse, and some headaches are associated with digital eyestrain, so giving your eyes a break can be beneficial.

RELAX EACH MUSCLE. Progressive muscle relaxation can also help. To give it a try, focus on a body part — say, your foot: Inhale and squeeze, curling your toes and tensing as hard as you can for about 8 seconds. Then exhale and relax your foot. Move up your body, part by part, to your face, repeating with different muscles.

DISTRACT YOURSELF. Engaging each of your senses (focusing on what you smell, hear, etc.) in a chill environment with a peaceful recording can divert your attention from the pain.

11 MONDAY

12 TUESDAY

13 WEDNESDAY ○

14 THURSDAY

15 FRIDAY

16 SATURDAY

17 SUNDAY

JULY 18-24
2022

M	T	W	T	F	S	S
				1	2	3
4	5	6	7	8	9	10
11	12	13	14	15	16	17
18	**19**	**20**	**21**	**22**	**23**	**24**
25	26	27	28	29	30	31

Whip Up Some Salsa

Nothing beats the bright flavor of fresh salsa—it's a crowd-pleaser for good reason. Even better, when you make your own, you can control the flavors. If you prefer less heat, make sure to remove the seeds from the jalapeños (or omit them altogether).

FRESH SALSA

Active **10 min.** | Total **10 min.**

- 2 jalapeños, finely chopped
- ½ small white onion, finely chopped
- 2 Tbsp lime juice
- ½ tsp salt
- ¼ tsp pepper
- 1 lb plum tomatoes, halved, seeded and chopped
- ½ cup chopped fresh cilantro
  Tortilla chips, for serving

1. In large bowl, toss jalapeños and onion with lime juice, salt and pepper; let sit 10 min.

2. Add tomatoes and cilantro. Toss gently. Serve with tortilla chips.

MAKES 3½ CUPS Per ½ cup, about 15 cal, 0 g fat (0 g sat), 1 g pro, 140 mg sodium, 4 g carb, 1 g fiber

18 MONDAY

19 TUESDAY

20 WEDNESDAY ◑

21 THURSDAY

22 FRIDAY

23 SATURDAY

24 SUNDAY

JULY 25-31

2022

M	T	W	T	F	S	S
				1	2	3
4	5	6	7	8	9	10
11	12	13	14	15	16	17
18	19	20	21	22	23	24
25	26	27	28	29	30	31

Get a Foolproof Self-Tan

A tan has the power to make you feel like you've just returned from a tropical vacation. It can camouflage "imperfections" like cellulite and varicose veins and make you appear thinner, if that's your goal. But who wants to bake in the sun's harmful rays for that elusive bronzed effect? Here's how to fake a sun-kissed glow without the risk of looking patchy or streaky.

1. DON'T apply after a shower. Instead, let skin dry completely before using the product. Hold off on body moisturizer too — it could form a barrier on skin that stops the tanner from developing evenly.

2. DO tread lightly. Slather it on dry skin. Go easy on areas of the body with dry skin, like the knees and elbows, as those spots can absorb the product faster, producing a darker color.

3. DON'T wait to fix mistakes. If you notice an "oops" like product overload or streaking in a specific spot, try to quickly blend it away with a makeup sponge or brush, or simply blot it with a paper towel.

25 MONDAY

26 TUESDAY

27 WEDNESDAY

28 THURSDAY ●

29 FRIDAY

30 SATURDAY

31 SUNDAY

AUGUST 2022

MONDAY	TUESDAY	WEDNESDAY	THURSDAY
1	2	3	4
8	9	10	11 ○
15	16	17	18
22	23	24	25
29	30	31	

FRIDAY	SATURDAY	SUNDAY
5 ◐	6	7
12	13	14
19 ◑	20	21
26	27 ●	28

Feel Good Goal

TRY SOMETHING NEW

Adventure is a state of mind, not a destination. This month, **find something you've always been curious to explore and make a plan for it to happen**. Sign up for a cooking class, get outdoors and find a trail you've never hiked before or try your hand at a new craft project. The point is to make it happen and enjoy yourself along the way.

JULY

M	T	W	T	F	S	S
				1	2	3
4	5	6	7	8	9	10
11	12	13	14	15	16	17
18	19	20	21	22	23	24
25	26	27	28	29	30	31

SEPTEMBER

M	T	W	T	F	S	S
			1	2	3	4
5	6	7	8	9	10	11
12	13	14	15	16	17	18
19	29	21	22	23	24	25
26	27	28	29	30		

AUGUST
1-7

2022

M	T	W	T	F	S	S
1	2	3	4	5	6	7
8	9	10	11	12	13	14
15	16	17	18	19	20	21
22	23	24	25	26	27	28
29	30	31				

"If you can dream it, you can do it."

— WALT DISNEY

1 MONDAY

2 TUESDAY

3 WEDNESDAY

4 THURSDAY

5 FRIDAY ☽

6 SATURDAY

7 SUNDAY

AUGUST 8-14
2022

M	T	W	T	F	S	S
1	2	3	4	5	6	7
8	9	10	11	12	13	14
15	16	17	18	19	20	21
22	23	24	25	26	27	28
29	30	31				

Be Daring in the Kitchen

Making a dish at home that you normally only order at a restaurant, like mussels, is an opportunity for adventure — not to mention that fresh seafood is so delicious on a warm summer evening!

WHITE WINE MUSSELS

Active **20 min.** | Total **20 min.**

- 2 Tbsp olive oil
- 4 cloves garlic, finely chopped
- ¼ tsp red pepper flakes
- 2 cups dry white wine
- ¼ tsp salt
- 4 lbs cleaned mussels
- 3 Tbsp cold butter
- ¼ cup chopped fresh parsley
  Crusty bread and lemon wedges, for serving

1. Heat oil with garlic and red pepper flakes in large Dutch oven on medium-low until beginning to turn golden brown, 4 min. Add wine and bring to a boil on medium-high, then boil 2 min.

2. Add salt, then mussels, and cook, covered, stirring once or twice, until shells open, 6 min. Uncover, add butter and cook 2 min., stirring. Toss with parsley and serve with crusty bread and lemon wedges if desired.

SERVES 4 About 280 cal, 18.5 g fat (7 g sat), 17 g pro, 515 mg sodium, 10 g carb, 0 g fiber

8 MONDAY

9 TUESDAY

10 WEDNESDAY

11 THURSDAY ○

12 FRIDAY

13 SATURDAY

14 SUNDAY

AUGUST 15–21

2022

M	T	W	T	F	S	S
1	2	3	4	5	6	7
8	9	10	11	12	13	14
15	**16**	**17**	**18**	**19**	**20**	**21**
22	23	24	25	26	27	28
29	30	31				

Wear Sun-Safe Gear

If your summer adventures involve outdoor activities, keep in mind that while sunscreen is a crucial part of protecting skin, it's not enough on its own. It's just as important to:

PUT ON SUN-SAFE CLOTHING and UV-blocking sunglasses. A wide-brimmed hat is also essential, especially since "about 10% of melanomas occur on the scalp," says Dendy Engelman, M.D., a board-certified dermatologist and Mohs micrographic surgeon in New York City.

SEEK SHADE during peak ray intensity (10 a.m. to 4 p.m.) whenever possible.

PROTECT YOURSELF WITH SPF YEAR-ROUND. Though we tend to focus on sun exposure in the summer, the reality is that up to 80% of UV rays can also get reflected off the surface of snow and seep through heavy cloud cover. And whatever the season, "windows at home and on trains, planes and cars allow UVA rays to pass through," Dr. Engelman explains.

15 MONDAY

16 TUESDAY

17 WEDNESDAY

18 THURSDAY

19 FRIDAY ☽

20 SATURDAY

21 SUNDAY

AUGUST 22-28
2022

M	T	W	T	F	S	S
1	2	3	4	5	6	7
8	9	10	11	12	13	14
15	16	17	18	19	20	21
22	**23**	**24**	**25**	**26**	**27**	**28**
29	30	31				

Pretty Up Your Porch

It's the perfect spot to lounge and learn new things about your friends over a cold cocktail. Add inviting flair with these tips:

INTRODUCE CONTRAST. Pair a wood dining table with cane chairs for a look that's equal parts modern and retro.

HANG A GLOBE CHANDELIER. Balance a rectangular table and wood accents with a round metal light fixture.

ADD FLOWERS AND GREENERY. Play up your room's transitional vibe by weaving in flower arrangements and potted plants.

TRY THIS TO FEEL
···· CALM ····

*Surround yourself with plants that allow you to **savor a soothing scent**. Lavender, chamomile, lemon balm and peppermint are all easy-to-grow options.*

22 MONDAY

23 TUESDAY

24 WEDNESDAY

25 THURSDAY

26 FRIDAY

27 SATURDAY ○

28 SUNDAY

SEPTEMBER 2022

MONDAY	TUESDAY	WEDNESDAY	THURSDAY
			1
5 Labor Day	**6**	**7**	**8**
12	**13**	**14**	**15**
19	**20**	**21**	**22** First Day of Fall
26	**27**	**28**	**29**

FRIDAY	SATURDAY	SUNDAY
2	**3** ◑	**4**
9	**10** ○	**11**
16	**17** ◐	**18**
23	**24**	**25** Rosh Hashanah ●
30		

Feel
Good
Goal

STREAMLINE AND SIMPLIFY

Clear your mind— and your living room. Taking to the sofa cushions with a vacuum attachment has multiple stress-reducing benefits on top of keeping you from hearing a mysterious crunch when you sit down. Any kind of cleaning requires a little planning and some physical activity, which is likely to result in a sense of achievement.

Doing it mindfully can reduce stress even more: One study in *Mindfulness* found that folks who were told to stay gently focused on what they were doing while washing dishes had boosts in positive feelings.

AUGUST

M	T	W	T	F	S	S
1	2	3	4	5	6	7
8	9	10	11	12	13	14
15	16	17	18	19	20	21
22	23	24	25	26	27	28
29	30	31				

OCTOBER

M	T	W	T	F	S	S
					1	2
3	4	5	6	7	8	9
10	11	12	13	14	15	16
17	18	19	20	21	22	23
24	25	26	27	28	29	30
31						

AUGUST 29– SEPTEMBER 4

2022

M	T	W	T	F	S	S
29	30	31	1	2	3	4
5	6	7	8	9	10	11
12	13	14	15	16	17	18
19	20	21	22	23	24	25
26	27	28	29	30		

"Adopt the pace of nature: her secret is patience."

—RALPH WALDO EMERSON

29 MONDAY

30 TUESDAY

31 WEDNESDAY

1 THURSDAY

2 FRIDAY

3 SATURDAY ☽

4 SUNDAY

SEPTEMBER 5-11

2022

M	T	W	T	F	S	S
			1	2	3	4
5	6	7	8	9	10	11
12	13	14	15	16	17	18
19	20	21	22	23	24	25
26	27	28	29	30		

Liven Up Your Next Walk

Some family activities can help you streamline your life by accomplishing two goals at once—like providing time for togetherness while also encouraging fitness. Jazz up a stroll with activities that engage your kids' creativity.

TALLY TEXTURES. Explore nature's variety by keeping track of how many different textures you can find. Look for items that are rough, soft, prickly and so on.

PLAY CRITTER COPYCAT. This active game lets you talk about the animals that share the planet with us.

GO ON A SCAVENGER HUNT FOR SOUNDS. Every so often, stop walking, ask everyone to close their eyes and listen. You might hear a bird calling, wind in the trees or an airplane flying overhead. Actively listening encourages a whole new appreciation for what's around you.

CREATE OUTDOOR ART. Arrange sticks, leaves, pinecones and other flora you find into interesting sculptures and shapes. If you're in an urban or suburban setting, post inspiring messages, silly jokes or sweet drawings in your street-facing windows for your neighbors to enjoy.

5 MONDAY Labor Day

6 TUESDAY

7 WEDNESDAY

8 THURSDAY

9 FRIDAY

10 SATURDAY ○

11 SUNDAY

SEPTEMBER 12-18
2022

M	T	W	T	F	S	S
			1	2	3	4
5	6	7	8	9	10	11
12	13	14	15	16	17	18
19	20	21	22	23	24	25
26	27	28	29	30		

Enjoy a Perfect Pairing

Pork chops are a fast, lean dinner option perfect for busy weeknights. This dish combines the sweetness of cherries with fresh spinach for a perfect one-pan meal.

SEARED PORK CHOPS WITH CHERRIES AND SPINACH

Active **15 min.** | Total **30 min.**

- 1 Tbsp olive oil
- 4 6-oz boneless pork chops
- ½ tsp each salt and pepper
- 1 cup cherries, pitted and halved
- ¼ cup dry white wine
- 2 tsp whole-grain mustard
- 2 bunches spinach, thick stems discarded

1. Heat oil in large skillet on medium. Pat pork chops dry with paper towel and season with salt and pepper. Cook until golden brown and just cooked through, 8 to 10 min. per side; transfer to plates.
2. Add cherries to skillet and cook, stirring occasionally, until beginning to soften, about 2 min. Add wine and cook until reduced to 1 Tbsp, about 2 min. more.
3. Stir in mustard and ⅓ cup water, then spinach, and cook, tossing, until beginning to wilt, 2 min. Serve with pork.

SERVES 4 About 450 cal, 28 g fat (9 g sat), 38 g pro, 450 mg sodium, 12 g carb, 4 g fiber

12 MONDAY

13 TUESDAY

14 WEDNESDAY

15 THURSDAY

16 FRIDAY

17 SATURDAY ◑

18 SUNDAY

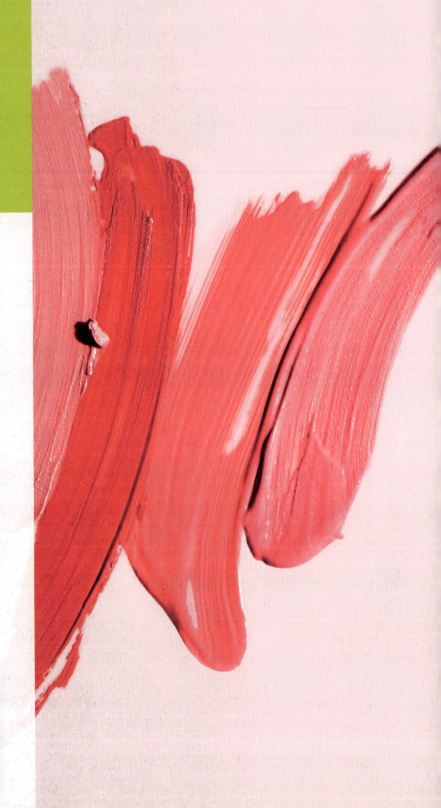

SEPTEMBER 19-25
2022

M	T	W	T	F	S	S
			1	2	3	4
5	6	7	8	9	10	11
12	13	14	15	16	17	18
19	**20**	**21**	**22**	**23**	**24**	**25**
26	27	28	29	30		

Get Gorgeous With One Do-It-All Product

You probably already know how to apply blush to your cheeks, but did you know that you can wear it on the rest of your face too? Yep, you can dab some on your eyes, cheeks and lips — it's a triple beauty threat.

CHEEKS Blend cream blush onto your cheeks, sweeping the blush from the cheekbones up to the hairline using a loose synthetic brush.

EYES Use what's left over on your finger to dab it on your eyelid, blending upward toward the brow. Avoid putting any color next to your lash line — you don't want to wind up looking sick.

LIPS Take more blush on your finger and press it to the center of your lips, blending out. Finish off with a swipe of your favorite lip balm, and you're all done!

TRY THIS TO FEEL
•••• CALM ••••

*Hit the snooze button one too many times? Having a **simplified skincare routine** can help with beating the stress of the morning rush. Find a cleanser and moisturizer that you know work for you, and keep them at the core of your routine.*

19 MONDAY

20 TUESDAY

21 WEDNESDAY

22 THURSDAY First Day of Fall

23 FRIDAY

24 SATURDAY

25 SUNDAY ● Rosh Hashanah

Inspiring Ways to Relax This
FALL

Transform your house into a place meant for lounging, making it a haven in the cool weather ahead— a place you really want to be.

Not every houseplant requires a natural green thumb. *Working with a dark room? Give* **low-light options** *like pothos, prayer plants and dracaena a go. Have a beautiful sunroom? Opt for* **ones that soak up the rays** *like yucca, jade and ponytail palm. Peace lilies and Chinese evergreen can handle the well-meaning over-waterer. If you're the* **set-it-and-forget-it** *type, ZZ plant, kalanchoe and philodendrons might be more your speed.*

DO A
Fall
"Fix-Up"

Though spring cleaning gets all the attention, fall is a great time to do a quick pass-through. All you need is to follow these three simple steps:

TACKLE THE MESS. Hit any spaces where clutter tends to accumulate—your closets, the family command center or your home office. Make two piles: one to toss, one to donate.

SPIFF UP ITEMS THAT GATHER A LOT OF DUST. Break out your long-handled duster to scour pendant lights and sconces, strip caked-on dust from ceiling fans with a pillowcase and use your vacuum's special attachments to give upholstery a once-over.

MAKE IT SPARKLE. Clean and disinfect surfaces—counters, doorknobs and handles. Cleaning wipes make quick work of this task.

Tap Into a Fall-Appropriate Color Palette

Find ways to incorporate rich, autumnal hues into your space—think oranges, greens and browns, says Monique Valeris, senior home editor for *Good Housekeeping*. And, no, that doesn't necessarily mean you have to spend a ton of money on new decor pieces.

There are plenty of easy ways to breathe new life into your space on a budget. Cozy up couches and chairs with extra blankets and throw pillows or try swapping out any art prints that have a beachy vibe for something more appropriate for the season.

You can also bring some natural autumnal elements indoors. For example, pop some pinecones into a pretty wooden bowl and display it on your coffee table. A potted plant is a great way to do this too. And studies suggest that plants not only help purify the air, but also boost overall happiness.

PUT SOMETHING COZY UNDERFOOT

There's nothing quite as chill-inducing as stepping out of a cozy, warm bed onto an ice-cold floor.

PLACE A SOFT RUG UNDER YOUR BED. You can also opt for runners on either side of it.

CONSIDER THE CONCEPT OF LAYERING. You can make a big design impact by layering a sisal rug with a patterned design, for example.

ADD A DECORATIVE MAT. Place it in your main space, especially near the entryway, because nobody wants wet, muddy footprints tracked throughout the house. You can also try a washable rug for this.

CONSIDER ALTERNATE LIGHTING

When the days are so short and darkness creeps in at an unnaturally early hour, you'll need sufficient lighting. But nix the harsh overheads. If you have recessed lighting, swap bright bulbs for smart LEDs — you can use your smartphone or set up voice command via a smart home hub to dim them, set timers and even change the color of the light. Also consider replacing any bright white lights in lamps with softer warm-toned lights.

Candles are another way to cast a cozy glow in your home once the sun goes down. They come in so many great fall scents like pumpkin and patchouli, and they set the mood and are great for entertaining.

STOCK UP ON COOKING ESSENTIALS

While you're in purge mode, take a peek inside your pantry. Toss expired goods and donate anything that's still good but that has remained untouched for months. Then take stock and craft a shopping list. Make sure you have everything you'll need for multipurpose cooking—think olive oil, salt and pepper, beans, grains like rice and pasta, and of course flour and sugar.

Bake Something Delicious

CHOCOLATE PUMPKIN BREAD

Active **25 min.** | Total **1 hr. 10 min. plus cooling**

Fragrant fresh ginger, warming pumpkin pie spice and a splash of vanilla extract amp up the festive flavor of an autumnal classic. Bittersweet chocolate chips give this treat just the right twist.

1⅓ cups all-purpose flour
1 tsp baking powder
½ tsp baking soda
1½ tsp pumpkin pie spice
½ tsp kosher salt
½ cup (1 stick) unsalted butter, melted
1 cup canned pure pumpkin
½ cup granulated sugar
¼ cup packed brown sugar
2 large eggs
2 Tbsp milk
2 tsp grated fresh ginger
1 tsp pure vanilla extract
½ cup plus 2 Tbsp bittersweet chocolate chips

1. Heat oven to 350°F. Lightly coat 8 - by 4 -in. loaf pan with cooking spray. Line with parchment, leaving overhang on 2 long sides; lightly coat paper with cooking spray.
2. In large bowl, whisk together flour, baking powder, baking soda, pumpkin pie spice and salt.
3. Transfer melted butter to another large bowl and whisk in pumpkin and sugars (this will help cool it down if it is still hot). Whisk in eggs, milk, ginger and vanilla. Add flour mixture and mix to combine; fold in ½ cup chocolate chips.
4. Transfer mixture to prepared pan, scatter remaining 2 Tbsp chips on top and bake until wooden pick inserted into center comes out clean, 45 to 55 min.
5. Transfer pan to wire rack and let cool 10 min. before using parchment overhangs to transfer bread to rack to cool completely.

SERVES 8 TO 10 About 370 cal, 17.5 g fat (10 g sat), 6 g pro, 260 mg sodium, 46 g carb, 1 g fiber

OCTOBER 2022

MONDAY	TUESDAY	WEDNESDAY	THURSDAY
3	4 Yom Kippur Begins	5	6
10 Indigenous Peoples' Day	11	12	13
17 ◑	18	19	20
24 Diwali	25 ●	26	27
31 Halloween			

FRIDAY	SATURDAY	SUNDAY
	1	**2** ◐
7	**8**	**9** ○
14	**15**	**16**
21	**22**	**23**
28	**29**	**30**

Feel Good Goal

FIND YOUR PASSION

In our productivity-obsessed society, it can be all too easy to get sucked into a routine cycle. But research shows that **cultivating hobbies isn't just a nice break for your body and brain** — it actually carries mental and physical health benefits. Of course, finding a new hobby you enjoy can feel like just another thing to add to your to-do list. So instead make it social. Call a friend and set out to improve your health and your outlook on the world.

SEPTEMBER

M	T	W	T	F	S	S
			1	2	3	4
5	6	7	8	9	10	11
12	13	14	15	16	17	18
19	29	21	22	23	24	25
26	27	28	29	30		

NOVEMBER

M	T	W	T	F	S	S
	1	2	3	4	5	6
7	8	9	10	11	12	13
14	15	16	17	18	19	20
21	22	23	24	25	26	27
28	29	30				

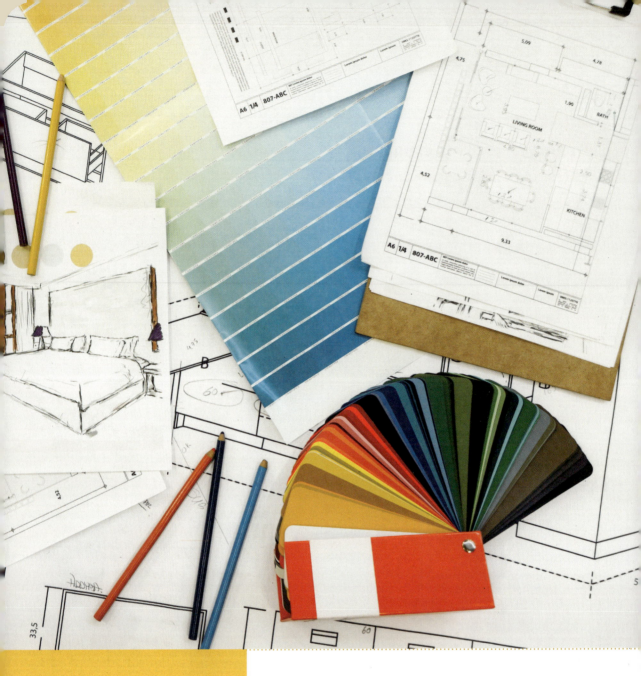

SEPTEMBER 26–
OCTOBER 2

2022

M	T	W	T	F	S	S
26	27	28	29	30	1	2
3	4	5	6	7	8	9
10	11	12	13	14	15	16
17	18	19	20	21	22	23
24	25	26	27	28	29	30
31						

"Everything you can imagine is real."

— PABLO PICASSO

26 MONDAY

27 TUESDAY

28 WEDNESDAY

29 THURSDAY

30 FRIDAY

1 SATURDAY

2 SUNDAY ◑

OCTOBER 3-9

2022

M	T	W	T	F	S	S
					1	2
3	4	5	6	7	8	9
10	11	12	13	14	15	16
17	18	19	20	21	22	23
24	25	26	27	28	29	30
31						

Have a Boo-tiful Halloween

Dream up a dramatic vignette in a carved pumpkin. Coat the inside with black craft paint, then fill the space with reindeer moss, twigs, jade plants, a faux pumpkin and mini headstones. Don't forget the full moon (hang a Ping-Pong ball from a thin string).

1. **Draw a circle** on the front of a pumpkin, at least 3" from the bottom. Use a pumpkin carving knife to carefully cut out the circle.

2. **Paint the inside** of the pumpkin with black craft paint and let it dry completely.

3. **Place self-adhesive** rhinestones inside the pumpkin to create a starry night sky.

4. **Spread a layer** of gravel or small rocks/pebbles in the bottom of the pumpkin to allow drainage. Fill the pumpkin with potting soil.

5. **Plant small succulents** and stick in some twig "trees." Add moss for color.

6. **Use a permanent marker** to write headstone messages or dates on small, flat rocks and nestle them into your scene.

7. **Lightly water** or mist the succulents once a week.

3 MONDAY

4 TUESDAY Yom Kippur Begins

5 WEDNESDAY

6 THURSDAY

7 FRIDAY

8 SATURDAY

9 SUNDAY ○

OCTOBER 10-16

2022

M	T	W	T	F	S	S
					1	2
3	4	5	6	7	8	9
10	11	12	13	14	15	16
17	18	19	20	21	22	23
24	25	26	27	28	29	30
31						

Make Your Own Pastry Dough

With the help of your trusty food processor, this buttery dough is easy as pie. Add flavor to this simple recipe by trying out flavor variations. One of our faves is Savory Thyme Pastry Dough—to make, skip the sugar in this recipe and add a tablespoon of thyme leaves instead.

EASIEST EVER PASTRY DOUGH

1¼ cups all-purpose flour
1 Tbsp sugar
½ tsp kosher salt
½ cup cold unsalted butter, cut up (1 stick)
1 Tbsp distilled white vinegar
1 Tbsp ice-cold water, plus 1 to 2 tsp more if necessary

1. In food processor, combine flour, sugar and salt. Add butter and pulse until mixture resembles coarse crumbs.
2. Add vinegar and 1 Tbsp ice-cold water, pulsing until dough is crumbly but holds together when squeezed (if necessary, add remaining water 1 tsp at a time). Do not overmix.
3. Transfer dough to piece of plastic wrap and shape into 1-in.-thick disk. Wrap tightly and refrigerate until firm, at least 1 hr and up to 2 days.

10 MONDAY Indigenous Peoples' Day

11 TUESDAY

12 WEDNESDAY

13 THURSDAY

14 FRIDAY

15 SATURDAY

16 SUNDAY

OCTOBER 17-23
2022

M	T	W	T	F	S	S
				1	2	
3	4	5	6	7	8	9
10	11	12	13	14	15	16
17	**18**	**19**	**20**	**21**	**22**	**23**
24	25	26	27	28	29	30
31						

Build Bouquets Like a Pro

Creating your own floral arrangements is a hobby that will bring as much joy to you as to the hostess, sick friend or birthday girl you gift them to. Not sure where to start? Buy and arrange a dozen colorful blooms with these pro tips in mind.

SET THE TONE WITH COLOR. Reach for a mix of tonal options — classic white or a bright assembly of warmer hues — for a cohesive arrangement. Personalize it with pops of unexpected color.

FOCUS ON BALANCE. The key to ensuring that your bouquet lives harmoniously with either you or its recipient is balance. Complement any space with tightly arranged bouquets cut closer to the vase.

CONSIDER ALL THE SENSES. A flower's fragrance can also influence our sense of taste. Consider blossoms of lavender, daisies, carnations and dahlias, which tend to work well with most dishes and can add additional dimension to the eating experience.

TRY THIS TO FEEL
• • • • CALM • • • •
Place a small vase in every room and use the process of **changing out the flowers weekly** *as a calming ritual.*

17 MONDAY ☽

18 TUESDAY

19 WEDNESDAY

20 THURSDAY

21 FRIDAY

22 SATURDAY

23 SUNDAY

M	T	W	T	F	S	S
				1	2	
3	4	5	6	7	8	9
10	11	12	13	14	15	16
17	18	19	20	21	22	23
24	25	26	27	28	29	30
31						

Shine New Light on an Old Lampshade

Dated lampshades can be combined to make a single rustic Scandi pendant.

STEP 1: PREP
Remove fabric and lining from a pair of matching shades and attach wire frames bottom to bottom with electrical tape. Pick a tape color that will blend.

STEP 2: LIGHT
Thread a pendant light cord through the middle and screw in an LED bulb, which won't get hot!

STEP 3: COVER
Hot-glue the end of a length of jute cord, twine or colored embroidery thread to top frame and wrap around until covered. Repeat with bottom half.

24 MONDAY Diwali

25 TUESDAY ●

26 WEDNESDAY

27 THURSDAY

28 FRIDAY

29 SATURDAY

30 SUNDAY

NOVEMBER 2022

MONDAY	TUESDAY	WEDNESDAY	THURSDAY
	1 All Saints Day ◑	**2**	**3**
7	**8** ○	**9**	**10**
14	**15**	**16** ◐	**17**
21	**22**	**23** ●	**24** Thanksgiving
28	**29**	**30** ◑	

FRIDAY	SATURDAY	SUNDAY
4	**5**	**6** Daylight Savings Time Ends
11 Veterans Day	**12**	**13**
18	**19**	**20**
25	**26**	**27** First Day of Advent

PRACTICE GRATITUDE

Treat joy as if it's finite. The awareness of an ending encourages us to **seize the moment while it lasts**. Acknowledging that holiday preparation and decorations have a very definite end point and your extended family will go home (Sob! But also, phew!) can help you treasure all of it even more.

OCTOBER

M	T	W	T	F	S	S
					1	2
3	4	5	6	7	8	9
10	11	12	13	14	15	16
17	18	19	20	21	22	23
24	25	26	27	28	29	30
31						

DECEMBER

M	T	W	T	F	S	S
			1	2	3	4
5	6	7	8	9	10	11
12	13	14	15	16	17	18
19	20	21	22	23	24	25
26	27	28	29	30	31	

OCTOBER 31–
NOVEMBER 6

2022

M	T	W	T	F	S	S
31	1	2	3	4	5	6
7	8	9	10	11	12	13
14	15	16	17	18	19	20
21	22	23	24	25	26	27
28	29	30				

"Peace begins with a smile."

—MOTHER TERESA

31 MONDAY Halloween

1 TUESDAY ◑ All Saints Day

2 WEDNESDAY

3 THURSDAY

4 FRIDAY

5 SATURDAY

6 SUNDAY Daylight Savings Time Ends

NOVEMBER 7-13
2022

M	T	W	T	F	S	S
	1	2	3	4	5	6
7	**8**	**9**	**10**	**11**	**12**	**13**
14	15	16	17	18	19	20
21	22	23	24	25	26	27
28	29	30				

Make a Thankfulness Tree

There's nothing like a gratitude tree to truly capture the spirit of the Thanksgiving season. It's a great tradition that involves having your guests write down what they're most thankful for on an ornament and placing them on the tree. More than a holiday decor piece and a handy conversation starter, it's also a wonderful way to feel more thankful. Here's how to start your own tradition:

1. **Spray paint some branches** — or leave them looking natural if you prefer — and arrange them in a colorful vase.

2. **Consider plain construction paper**, kraft paper or any materials you have handy for the leaves. Try scrapbooking paper if you're feeling fancy.

3. **Decide how to hang them** — tiny clothespins or twine works nicely.

TRY THIS TO FEEL
•••• CALM ••••

*Ground yourself in difficult times by writing down five things you're grateful for. "**The trick is to get specific**," says mindset coach Shirin Eskandani. "Instead of 'I am grateful for family,' try: 'I am grateful for the Zoom call I had with my parents and sister last night."*

7 MONDAY

8 TUESDAY ○

9 WEDNESDAY

10 THURSDAY

11 FRIDAY Veterans Day

12 SATURDAY

13 SUNDAY

NOVEMBER 14-20

2022

M	T	W	T	F	S	S
	1	2	3	4	5	6
7	8	9	10	11	12	13
14	**15**	**16**	**17**	**18**	**19**	**20**
21	22	23	24	25	26	27
28	29	30				

Reimagine Your Holiday Favorites

Sometimes the old standard holiday recipes deserve a fresh perspective. Here's one to try that will definitely spice things up.

MUSHROOM & CHILE-GARLIC GREEN BEANS

Active **10 min.** | Total **35 min.**

- 1 lb mixed wild mushrooms
- 1 Tbsp olive oil
- ¼ tsp each salt and pepper
- 1 lb green beans
- 4 Tbsp unsalted butter
- 2 cloves garlic, thinly sliced
- 1 red chile, thinly sliced

1. Heat oven to 450°F. On rimmed baking sheet, toss mushrooms with oil and salt and pepper and roast until golden brown and tender, about 25 min.

2. Meanwhile, blanch green beans and transfer to a large bowl.

3. In a small pan, melt butter with garlic and chile on low, then cook until golden brown, 10 min. Toss beans with garlic butter and mushrooms.

SERVES 8 About 105 cal, 8 g fat (4 g sat), 3 g pro, 115 mg sodium, 8 g carb, 3 g fiber

14 MONDAY

15 TUESDAY

16 WEDNESDAY ◑

17 THURSDAY

18 FRIDAY

19 SATURDAY

20 SUNDAY

NOVEMBER 21-27
2022

M	T	W	T	F	S	S
	1	2	3	4	5	6
7	8	9	10	11	12	13
14	15	16	17	18	19	20
21	22	23	24	25	26	27
28	29	30				

Eat to Boost Your Immunity

Good health is definitely something to be grateful for as the holiday season nears. Here are the foods that can keep you in top shape:

PROBIOTIC FOODS: Fermented foods like yogurt and sauerkraut support good gut bacteria. These beneficial microorganisms can boost natural antibodies that help fight infection.

PROTEIN: Legumes and lean animal protein sources help build and repair tissues that support a healthy immune system. Meat, shellfish and legumes supply zinc, a mineral that helps heal wounds.

FRUITS AND VEGGIES: Citrus, strawberries, sweet potatoes and other produce that contain vitamins C and A can protect the integrity of immune cells. The fiber in these also supports good gut bacteria.

NUTS: Almonds, hazelnuts, peanuts and nut butters contain vitamin E, an antioxidant that can help protect against several infectious diseases.

WATER: Flushing out toxins that wreak havoc on your immune cells requires a lot of water. Start with an extra 2 cups of water a day and build up. Soup counts; skip sugary fruit juices.

21 MONDAY

22 TUESDAY

23 WEDNESDAY ●

24 THURSDAY Thanksgiving

25 FRIDAY

26 SATURDAY

27 SUNDAY First Day of Advent

DECEMBER 2022

MONDAY	TUESDAY	WEDNESDAY	THURSDAY
			1
5	**6**	**7** ○	**8**
12	**13**	**14**	**15**
19	**20**	**21** First Day of Winter	**22**
26 First Day of Kwanzaa	**27**	**28**	**29** ◐

FRIDAY	SATURDAY	SUNDAY
2	**3**	**4**
9	**10**	**11**
16 ◐	**17**	**18** Hanukkah Begins
23 ●	**24** Christmas Eve	**25** Christmas Day
30	**31** New Year's Eve	

Feel Good Goal

MAKE EVERY MOMENT COUNT

Practice becoming aware. Getting out of your head and into your senses can bring you back to the here and now, restoring a feeling of calm. Try this quick exercise: Ask yourself, "What's one thing I can smell, one thing I can taste, one thing I can touch?" **Activating all the senses is a good grounding technique** to help you focus on what's literally right under your nose.

NOVEMBER

M	T	W	T	F	S	S
	1	2	3	4	5	6
7	8	9	10	11	12	13
14	15	16	17	18	19	20
21	22	23	24	25	26	27
28	29	30				

JANUARY

M	T	W	T	F	S	S
						1
2	3	4	5	6	7	8
9	10	11	12	13	14	15
16	17	18	19	20	21	22
23	24	25	26	27	28	29
30	31					

M	T	W	T	F	S	S
28	29	30	1	2	3	4
5	6	7	8	9	10	11
12	13	14	15	16	17	18
19	20	21	22	23	24	25
26	27	28	29	30	31	

"The little things? The little moments? They aren't little."

— JON KABAT-ZINN

28 MONDAY

29 TUESDAY

30 WEDNESDAY ◑

1 THURSDAY

2 FRIDAY

3 SATURDAY

4 SUNDAY

DECEMBER 5-11

2022

M	T	W	T	F	S	S
			1	2	3	4
5	6	7	8	9	10	11
12	13	14	15	16	17	18
19	20	21	22	23	24	25
26	27	28	29	30	31	

Whip Up Easy Treats

Need a quick homemade gift to share? Keep a bag of hard peppermint candies on hand so you're just minutes away from a colorful treat that's sure to inspire smiles.

FESTIVE PEPPERMINT TREES

1. Heat oven to 350°F. Coat insides of metal Christmas tree cookie cutters with **nonstick cooking spray** and place on parchment-lined baking sheet.

2. Arrange **green peppermint candies** (breaking them as necessary) inside cutters; there should be a space between candies.

3. Bake until candies melt, 5 to 6 min. Let cool completely, then gently pop out.

TRY THIS TO FEEL
···• CALM •···

*While candy is probably not the best **antidote for an upset stomach**, a cup of peppermint tea can do the trick if holiday stress has you in overdrive.*

5 MONDAY

6 TUESDAY

7 WEDNESDAY ○

8 THURSDAY

9 FRIDAY

10 SATURDAY

11 SUNDAY

DECEMBER 12-18
2022

M	T	W	T	F	S	S
			1	2	3	4
5	6	7	8	9	10	11
12	**13**	**14**	**15**	**16**	**17**	**18**
19	20	21	22	23	24	25
26	27	28	29	30	31	

Use the Fancy Plates

Any time you get to spend with loved ones is a "special occasion," so go ahead and pull out your grandmother's heirloom china. Here are some tips for taking care when it's time to clean up:

HAND-WASH. Your dishwasher probably has a delicate spray setting for china, but in this case the experts at our GH Cleaning Lab wouldn't recommend it, especially if the pattern has a raised design that's applied on top of the glaze. Instead, put on a pair of rubber gloves to make sure you have a secure grip and hand-wash one plate at a time in a plastic basin of warm, sudsy water.

USE A SOFT CLOTH OR SPONGE. Then rinse, being careful not to let the plate hit the faucet. Set each plate to drain in a rack before washing the next one.

PROTECT THEM FROM CHIPPING. Never stack your china in the sink or have any items, like utensils, in the basin. If you prefer to wash the plates under running water, lay a towel in the sink for cushioning. Hand-dry your set and store in zippered quilted bags.

12 MONDAY

13 TUESDAY

14 WEDNESDAY

15 THURSDAY

16 FRIDAY ◐

17 SATURDAY

18 SUNDAY Hanukkah Begins

DECEMBER 19-25
2022

M	T	W	T	F	S	S
			1	2	3	4
5	6	7	8	9	10	11
12	13	14	15	16	17	18
19	**20**	**21**	**22**	**23**	**24**	**25**
26	27	28	29	30	31	

Feel More Joy This Season

The secret is a technique psychologists call savoring, a way to fully absorb life's special moments. Try out these expert tricks:

CELEBRATE EARLY. Stores that stock holiday decor in the fall have the right idea. Thinking about and planning a holiday extends its bliss beyond a few short weeks.

HAVE AN INTERMISSION. Take a break in the middle of gift giving or wait an hour before serving dessert. Even a brief hiatus from something enjoyable can reset your pleasure level.

CREATE MINI TRADITIONS. Engaging in a short ritual before doing something you like can make your experience even better. Find ways to turn tree decorating into a fun routine you can truly savor at every step.

TAKE A PHOTO . . . IN YOUR HEAD. Snapping a mental picture of an unexpected delight, like your kid's face as she bites into a gingerbread cookie, can help instantly rekindle positive emotions later.

19 MONDAY

20 TUESDAY

21 WEDNESDAY First Day of Winter

22 THURSDAY

23 FRIDAY ●

24 SATURDAY Christmas Eve

25 SUNDAY Christmas Day

DECEMBER 26– JANUARY 1
2022-2023

M	T	W	T	F	S	S
			1	2	3	4
5	6	7	8	9	10	11
12	13	14	15	16	17	18
19	20	21	22	23	24	25
26	27	28	29	30	31	1

Pick a 30-Day Challenge

If December is always so extra — as in extra drinking, extra eating or extra spending — January offers the chance to issue a corrective. It's no wonder that people wait until the new year to take on monthlong challenges like Whole30 or Dry January. If you have a mini goal that you don't think is right for a year-long resolution, plan to get it out of the way that first month and start setting yourself up now to stick with it.

To firm your resolve, share your intention with someone or ask them to join you in the challenge. Who knows where it could lead you?

TRY THIS TO FEEL
••• CALM •••

*When you wake up **practice a few minutes of positive affirmations** to mentally steel yourself. Repeat a favorite mantra, set your intentions for the day ahead, or record your goals using the free ThinkUp app. According to research, using a phone app can boost the likelihood that your new habits will stick.*

26 **MONDAY** First Day of Kwanzaa

27 **TUESDAY**

28 **WEDNESDAY**

29 **THURSDAY** ◑

30 **FRIDAY**

31 **SATURDAY** New Year's Eve

1 **SUNDAY** New Year's Day

Thank You

PHOTO CREDITS

(All Left to Right/Top to Bottom)